OSPREY AIRCRAFT OF THE ACES • 111

Russian Aces of World War 1

SERIES EDITOR: TONY HOLMES

OSPREY AIRCRAFT OF THE ACES • 111

Russian Aces of World War 1

Victor Kulikov

OSPREY
PUBLISHING

Front Cover

In early 1915 several Russian aviators attempted to install more effective armament in their aeroplanes than the pistols or rifles usually used in encounters with enemy aircraft. Poruchik Alexander Kozakov conceived an explosive entanglement system which he deployed below his Morane-Saulnier Type G, MS316. A small sea anchor was unreeled on a cable, then blocks of gunpowder were lowered to the cable's end. After diving upon the enemy aircraft and snaring it with the anchor, the gunpowder would explode and destroy it.

Having tested his device in late March 1915, Kozakov took off on the 31st of that month in pursuit of an enemy aircraft. The flight ended 30 minutes later when he crash-landed near his own airfield at Guzov, Kozakov subsequently recalling;

'The damned drag anchor got caught and was dangling underneath the enemy aeroplane, so I decided to strike across the uppersurface of the Albatros with the undercarriage of my Morane. Without a moment's thought I pushed the elevator down and collided with the enemy. The undercarriage folded up into my fuselage and then something exploded with a loud whistling noise. Seconds later a piece of the Morane's wing struck my elbow. The Albatros rolled to one side, then folded its wings and dropped like a stone. I had switched off the engine because one blade of the propeller was missing. Having lost my bearings, I began gliding. It was only owing to the shrapnel bursts that I could guess where the Russian front was. At first I went down "parachuting", and even turned upside down, but near the earth I was able to correct my flight and land safely. The impact between the aircraft had been so strong that the Morane's undercarriage was curved inwards under the wings.'

Although Kozakov had destroyed the enemy aircraft, his anchor device had clearly failed and his Morane had sustained serious damage. Nonetheless, his comrades admired him for this daring encounter. In a report to the Russian 1st Army, the commanding officer of the 4th KAO stated 'This deed of selflessness must be regarded with great pride by those serving in Russian military aviation' (*cover artwork by Mark Postlethwaite*)

First published in Great Britain in 2013 by Osprey Publishing
Midland House, West Way, Botley, Oxford, OX2 0PH
43-01 21st Street, Suite 220B, Long Island City, NY, 11101, USA

E-mail; info@ospreypublishing.com

Osprey Publishing is part of the Osprey Group

A CIP catalogue record for this book is available from the British Library

ISBN: 978 1 78096 059 3
PDF e-book ISBN: 978 1 78096 060 9
e-Pub ISBN: 978 1 78096 061 6

Edited by Tony Holmes and Philip Jarrett
Cover Artwork by Mark Postlethwaite
Aircraft Profiles by Harry Dempsey
Index by Alan Thatcher
Originated by PDQ Digital Media Solutions, UK
Printed in China through Bookbuilders

13 14 15 16 17   10 9 8 7 6 5 4 3 2 1

Osprey Publishing is supporting the Woodland Trust, the UK's leading woodland conservation charity, by funding the dedication of trees.

www.ospreypublishing.com

CONTENTS

INTRODUCTION

Although it could be argued that aeronautics and aviation were still in their infancy in Russia when World War 1 commenced on 18 July 1914, the nation entered the conflict with the most powerful air arm among the belligerent countries, having more than 200 pilots and nearly as many aeroplanes. And in spite of the difficult conditions that prevailed in-theatre throughout the war, the Russian Army Aviation Service exerted considerable influence on military operations on the Eastern Front. The first Russian AOI (*Aviatsionniy Otryad Istrebitelei* – fighter aviation detachment) appeared at the front in the spring of 1916, and by war's end there were 15 fighter squadrons and four BAGs (*Boevaya Aviatsionnaya Gruppa* – battle aviation group) manned by more than 150 pilots.

Russian aviators developed many of the tactics used in aerial combat. They were also the first to resort to the technique of ramming hostile aircraft. They mastered formation flying, whereby fighters could escort bombers over enemy territory, as well as conducting long-range reconnaissance of the enemy's rear units. The selfless bravery, courage and skill of Russian pilots typically compensated for the often-imperfect techniques trialled in combat and then discarded after they had proven flawed.

Within the ranks of the Imperial Military Air Fleet were 13 pilots who each accounted for five or more aeroplanes destroyed to earn the title of ace – Alexander Kozakov (16 victories), Ivan Smirnov (ten victories), Vasily Yanchenko (nine victories), Grigory Suk (eight victories), Ivan Loiko (six victories) and Vladimir Strzhizhevsky, Evgraf Kruten, Konstantin Vakulovsky, Ivan Orlov, Yury Gilsher, Aleksandr Pishvanov, Nikolai Kokorin and Donat Makijonek, each with five victories. Pavel Argeev claimed three and three shared victories, plus nine while flying with the French *Aviation Militaire* in 1918.

In researching this book, the records in the Russian State Military Historical Archive, the Russian State Military Archive, the N E Zhukovsky Scientific-Memorial Museum and the M V Frunze Museum of Aviation and Cosmonautics have all been consulted. I offer my profound gratitude to Frank Dorber of Great Britain for his generous assistance. My thanks also go to Svetlana Nadtochy for assistance with the translation and Gennady Petrov and Mikhail Maslov for the provision of photographs.

FIGHTER AVIATION IN RUSSIA

The idea of fighting for aerial supremacy was discussed within the ranks of the Russian Army Aviation Service even before the commencement of World War 1. During the military manoeuvres of 1911 pilots were tasked with fighting the 'enemy's' air fleet. In September of that same year the Warsaw military district troops staged their annual manoeuvres, and pilots from the Sevastopol flying school took part. On 2 September an 'air fight' took place during the manoeuvres when an 'enemy' dirigible appeared above the 'Southern' forces in the field. Having noticed it, flying school pilots Dybovsky and Buksgevden immediately took off and 'attacked' the dirigible, flying above it several times. Umpires officiating during the manoeuvres noted that 'this was the first air attack since aeronautics had come into being'. Russian pilots were now convinced that it was possible to destroy an aerial enemy if the necessary armament was available.

Long before the war, forward-thinking Russian pilots tried to find practical ways and means of combating enemy aircraft. In 1913 Poruchik (Lieutenant) Poplavko mounted an infantry Maxim machine gun in the nose of a Farman XV cockpit, while well-known Russian military pilot Peter Nesterov worked out manoeuvres in the horizontal and vertical planes – the basis of aerobatics.

Indeed, it was Nesterov who, for the first time in aviation history, engaged in aerial combat. This historic event occurred on 26 August 1914 (this and other dates up to February 1918 are in the Julian calendar, which was 12 days behind the Gregorian (Western) calendar in the 19th century, and 13 days behind in the 20th century) when he rammed and brought down a two-seat Albatros B II of the 11th *Flieger Kompanie*. This proved to be a pyrrhic victory, however, as all the participants in the engagement

In 1913 Poruchik Poplavko fitted this Farman XV pusher with a Maxim machine gun at the Klement'evo firing ground. The ex-infantry weapon is seen here ready to be fired into gun butts. Poruchik V R Poplavko (wearing a flying helmet) explains how the weapon works to visiting senior officers

Commander of the 11th KAO, Shtabs-Kapitan Peter Nesterov rammed an Austro-Hungarian Albatros B II with his Morane-Saulnier Type G on 26 August 1914. Both he and the crew of the enemy machine perished in the collision

perished – German pilot Fw Franz Malina, his observer Oblt Friedrich Rosental and Shtabs-Kapitan (Staff-Captain) Peter Nesterov of the 11th KAO (*Korpusnoi Aviatsionniy Otryad* – Corps Aviation Detachment).

The urgent problem in Russian aviation during the initial war period was the absence of armament. The standard weaponry for its aircraft at the time was just two Mauser pistols, which were useless in the air, so Russian pilots sought ways of arming their machines. In early August 1914, when the 11th KAO was located at Dubno, the detachment's commander, Peter Nesterov, fitted a knife to the rear fuselage of his Morane-Saulnier Type G, intending to use it to slit the envelope of an enemy dirigible. In mid-August he attached a long weighted rope to his Nieuport IV, planning to entangle the propeller of an enemy machine by flying above and ahead of it. When he first tried to take off with this device, on 26 August, the rope broke. That is why, when Nesterov took off for the second time to pursue an enemy aeroplane, he decided to use the only reliable option available to him when it came to destroying the enemy – ramming.

The High Command's belated understanding of the necessity for armament with which to engage the enemy did not improve the situation. Only at the end of 1914 did the Russian Army begin to receive armed French Voisin biplanes, although the majority of the aircraft supplied remained unarmed during 1914-15. Therefore, during this period aerial combat rarely took place. At best, when opposing pilots met in the air they fired pistols or carbines at each other.

At the beginning of the year Poruchik Alexander Kozakov of the 4th KAO equipped his Morane-Saulnier Type G with a sea anchor fitted with a slab of gun cotton. He planned to fly above an enemy aeroplane, throw out the anchor on a rope, snare the aircraft and then set off the explosive. On 18 March 1915, near the village of Guzov, on the right bank of the River Vistula, Kozakov tried to use his device, but the rope became tangled so he decided to ram the German Albatros, which tumbled down and crashed. Kozakov managed to land his damaged aircraft. This was the first victory for Russia's future ranking ace.

In the first half of 1915 two detachments were formed within the Russian Army Aviation Service to engage German aircraft – one for the air defence of Warsaw and the other to guard the Imperial residence.

Having concentrated a considerable number of aeroplanes on the Russian-German front by the end of 1915, the German command arranged 'aircraft barriers' along the frontline with the aim of preventing Russian

Armed with Le Prieur rockets on its wing struts, this Nieuport 21 was assigned to the Grenadier aviation detachment. Vladimir Kaminsky and Vladimir Kvasnikov used this aircraft/rocket combination to shoot down three captive enemy balloons between June and September 1917

pilots from conducting aerial reconnaissance. But the Russians still attacked enemy aircraft, either destroying them or forcing them to turn back. Thus it was reported, 'At the front sector near Minsk five aeroplanes were shot down and captured during October 1915. Two damaged Albatros biplanes managed to land on the Russian side, and two Albatros and one "Taube" monoplane also landed there but suffered less damage. Five German pilots perished and six were captured during these operations'.

The struggle for aerial supremacy on the Russian Front became extremely fierce in the spring of 1916. By this time the fighter aviation units had already been organisationally detached from the reconnaissance units, in the form of special AOIs. Russia set about forming such units in March 1916, creating one fighter squadron for each army. This process took a whole year to complete owing to the lack of special fighter aircraft and trained pilots.

By the summer of 1916 the situation in the air on the Russian-German front had become even more complicated. The swift offensive by Russian troops on the Southwest Front compelled the German command to urgently transfer considerable land and air forces to the east. At the end of July the Head of aircraft and aeronautics in the Field Army reported to the General Headquarters that 'the Germans have concentrated on our front a great number of high-speed machines, mainly fighters. According to the testimony of prisoners, all of the new enemy aviation units have arrived from the Western Front, particularly out of Verdun'. Owing to their numerical and qualitative superiority, the German aircraft substantially limited the activity of Russian pilots on some sectors of the front. The struggle for supremacy in the air had become an important task for Russian pilots.

The shortage of aircraft made it impossible to achieve numerical superiority over the Germans, so it was necessary to find other ways to gain aerial supremacy. It was therefore proposed to concentrate the fighter units at decisive locations in the most important front sectors,

A synchronised Colt-Browning M1895 machine gun as fitted to a Russian Morane-Saulnier Type L scout

Nieuport 23 N3598 was issued to the 1st BAG's 19th KAO on 16 August 1917, and by 1 November it had flown 27 hours and 45 minutes in combat. Much of this was with Poruchik Boris Guber at the controls. In November 1917 the aeroplane was captured by Austro-Hungarian troops

Built in France and delivered to Moscow in July 1917, Nieuport 23 N3216 was sent to the front in September. It was issued to the 8th AOI on 12 October, where it was routinely flown by Podporuchik Konstantin Krauze (seen here standing in the centre of this group). This photograph was taken at Novolselitse airfield, Chernovtsy, southwest Ukraine, in October 1917

as experience had shown that single fighter squadrons equally distributed among the armies could not paralyse the activities of enemy aircraft and ensure the normal work of Russia's own reconnaissance units. For that reason it was decided to form fighter aviation groups known as BAGs, each of which was comprised of several KAOs. Such groups gave considerable support to the front command, influencing the situation in the air and achieving air superiority in important locations and sectors.

The 1st BAG was formed within the Russian Army in August 1916. It comprised the 2nd, 4th and 19th KAOs, all of which already had experience of aerial combat. The detachments retained their old titles and staff, but after becoming part of the 1st BAG and being rearmed, they became AOIs. Their main task was 'to engage with enemy pilots appearing over our positions, with the aim of safeguarding the latter from enemy raids and counteracting enemy reconnaissance'. In addition, the BAG had to escort army aeroplanes during reconnaissance of the enemy's rear positions and, in exceptional cases, carry out independent reconnaissance deep in the enemy's rear.

The 1st BAG of the Southwestern Front began operations not far from Lutsk in the second half of August 1916. Between 24 and 31 August (including three non-flying days due to poor weather) the group's pilots saw air combat 14 times, during which they shot down one enemy aeroplane and put several out of action, suffering no losses themselves. Consequently, German pilots attempted to operate in formations. Thus on 13 September a formation of 16 enemy aeroplanes tried to break through to Lutsk, but they were engaged by eight aeroplanes from the BAG. After fierce fighting the German aeroplanes, despite outnumbering their opponents two-to-one, were scattered and driven back over the frontline.

The results of the 1st BAG's intensive activity during this period were felt quickly.

The first AOIs had appeared on the Russian Front in June 1916, and by the end of the year there were 12 of them in the Russian Army. Because of the great extent of the frontline and the small number of fighters, their work was not very effective. The impossibility of quickly increasing the number of AOIs and the acute shortage of fighters to protect the aeroplanes of the army and KAOs caused the Russian Command to seek other

Nieuports of the 3rd BAG are prepared for their next mission at Dubno airfield on the Western Front. Nieuport 23 N3626, closest to the camera, was from the 22nd KAO

Left
Nieuport 17 N1963 of the 15th AOI of the 4th BAG in November 1917

solutions. Order No 1658 of December 1916, issued by the Supreme Headquarters Chief of Staff, prescribed 'start to form fighter and artillery sections comprising KAOs'.

The fighter sections of such Aviation Detachments numbered from one to three aeroplanes, and their main purpose was to accompany the detachment's aircraft during reconnaissance, photography and aerial spotting flights. Such an approach had definite advantages, as the few fighter AOIs could not provide sufficient protection for all the aeroplanes belonging to corps, army and artillery KAOs. The pilots of the fighter sections assigned to the individual detachments coped with these tasks, however.

Detrimentally, this new arrangement forced the Command to scatter its sparse fighter aviation forces equally between the detachments, instead of creating mobile and strong fighter aviation groups.

In 1917 the fighter aviation units continued to play an important role on the Eastern Front. But the insufficient quantity of fighters owing to the low output of the Russian aircraft industry and the modest numbers delivered from abroad meant that the strength of fighter aviation could not be greatly increased. In that year only three more fighter squadrons were formed – the 13th, 14th and 15th AOIs. In addition, two more BAGs were organised in the spring. The 2nd BAG, formed in April as a constituent of the XI Army on the Southwestern Front and comprised of the 3rd, 4th and 8th KAOs, was commanded by well-known Russian ace

Nieuport 17 (N4187) of the 22nd KAO was assigned to Starshyi Unter-Officer Kibasov, who flew it on the Western Front from August 1917

Kapitan (Captain) Evgraf Kruten. Simultaneously, on the Western Front, the 3rd BAG was formed. Consisting of the 1st, 11th and 22nd KAOs, it was led by Podpolkovnik (Lieutenant Colonel) Ivan Zemitan.

In June 1917 the 4th BAG was organised as part of the 5th Army on the Northern Front, the group consisting of the 5th, 13th, 14th and 15th AOIs. In August an attempt was made to create the 5th BAG from the 2nd, 6th and 7th AOIs, under the command of future ace Kapitan Pavel Argeev, but the disintegration of the front that followed the October Revolution and the chaos that subsequently gripped the nation during the great political changes sweeping across Russia prevented its formation.

Earlier that year the first publications on tactics written by Russian fighter pilots had appeared. *Material on Air Fighting Tactics* by Vyacheslav Tkachev, *Methods of Conducting Air Fighting* by Ivan Orlov (commander of the 7th AOI) and *Air Fighting* by Evgraf Kruten elaborated on the constituent elements of air fighting, defined the main steps towards achieving a victory, described aerobatic techniques used in air combat and made concrete recommendations for flying personnel. Of particular interest were Kruten's suggestions regarding a rational organisational structure of fighter aviation, the main characteristics of a successful fighter aeroplane and the establishment of a Russian school of air fighting tactics.

This SPAD VII served with the 3rd KAO of the 2nd BAG from September 1917. The pilot standing alongside the fighter is Sotnik (Cossack Lieutenant) Ya K Filonov

Progressive Russian fighter pilots laid the foundation for combining aerobatics and skilful manoeuvres with firing, and advanced the principle of offensive attacks. They formulated and proposed the main objectives of fighter aviation – to gain supremacy in the air, to escort ground troops and to enable the other aviation arms to work effectively.

- SYNCHRONISED MACHINE GUNS IN RUSSIA -

A key factor in the escalation of aerial combat in World War 1 was the invention of synchronising gear to allow a machine gun to be fired between the rotating blades of a propeller. Like their counterparts in western Europe, Russian engineers initially struggled to provide aviators in the frontline with such a device. A number of proposals were submitted to the Russian Army's Military-Technical Committee, some of which came very close to solving the problem. Success, however, was to ultimately be enjoyed by just one man.

In late 1915 Russian Navy Lieutenant Victor Dybovsky of the 20th KAO, who had been seconded to the Dux aircraft works, constructed an original device for firing a fixed machine gun through the propeller disc. The firing of the weapon was regulated by cam plates mounted on the engine crankshaft, which transmitted pressure to the machine gun's trigger mechanism at the appropriate moments. At the end of November 1915 factory tests of a Dybovsky synchronisation system for the Le Rhône rotary engine were successfully completed, and serial production was planned.

Morane-Saulnier Type G MS567, fitted with a synchronised Vickers gun, was sent from the Dux works to the 30th KAO of the IXth Army late in November. Pilot Poruchik Mikhail Shadsky of this detachment

The attempt made by the 7th KAO to change the Morane-Saulnier Type G into a fighter by mounting a Madsen automatic rifle so that it could shoot over the propeller can be clearly seen in this photograph. Sat in the cockpit of the machine is Praporshchik Alexander Sveshnikov, who was subsequently sent to France in November 1916 to gain combat experience over the Western Front

A far superior weapon to the Type G's Madsen – a Vickers 0.303-in synchronised machine gun fitted to a Nieuport 21

made the first trial flight of the aircraft on 9 December 1915, but after just 20 minutes he had to land at the airfield because frost had caused the gun's lubricating oil to thicken and the weapon would not work. The same happened during a flight on 29 December.

Testing of the Type G with its synchronised gun did not resume until April 1916, by which time the weather had greatly improved. During April and May Shadsky was involved in around ten aerial combats. On 23 May he attacked an enemy aeroplane and forced it to land in the Austrian rear area. The next day Shadsky shot down an enemy aircraft that according to eyewitnesses fell behind the lines of Austrian trenches. However, Shadsky himself perished during this encounter, having received fatal injuries. His aircraft, with its synchronised gun, was destroyed when it crashed.

Despite the great necessity for such an effective weapon, Russia failed to put Dybovsky's synchronising system into production. The inventor was soon sent on a mission to England by the Navy Department to inspect aeroplanes then under construction for the Royal Flying Corps (RFC). Whilst there he profitably sold his patent, upon which the highly successful Scarff-Dybovsky synchronisation system was subsequently based – this equipment was widely fitted to RFC fighters.

By 1 April 1917 Russian aviation had only about two-dozen fighters equipped with synchronised machine guns. Because of the acute shortage of synchroniser mechanisms, aviators tried to devise simpler devices for shooting through the propeller disc.

Pilot Praporshchik (Ensign) Victor Kulebakin of the 3rd KAO proposed steel deflectors for bullets, and these were installed on a Mosca aircraft works Morane-Saulnier Type G. Special cam-deflectors connected to the engine crankshaft appeared from under the bonnet just as the blades were passing in front of the muzzle, thus saving the propeller from damage. Ground and flight tests carried out in July 1917 at the Khodynka range in Moscow showed that Kulebakin's system worked faultlessly. There was no need to make alterations or changes to the engine, machine gun or aircraft when installing the deflectors, and the KAOs' workshops could cope with the installation. Unfortunately this invention was not widely used.

ACES OF THE 1st BAG

Alexander Kozakov

Alexander Kozakov was born on 2 January 1889 into a family of gentry in the Kherson region of Russia. He studied at the Military School in Voronezh until 1906, and on 30 June that year proceeded to the Cavalry School at Elizavethgrad. Exactly two years later, his training completed, he was posted to the 12th Uhlan Regiment of Belgorod with the rank of Kornet (Cornet). Ironically, this regiment was under the honorary command of the Austrian Emperor, Franz Josef. As the year in which Kozakov joined the unit was the 60th anniversary of the Emperor's reign, he was awarded a Silver Jubilee Medal and an Austrian Sash. Three years later he was promoted to Poruchik and began to take an interest in aviation and the new airfields that were opening up across the Russian empire.

Kozakov's official request to be sent to the Aviation Department of the Officers' Aeronautic School (later known as Gatchinskaya Military Flying School) at Gatchina to study 'piloting' was accepted and he arrived there on 23 January 1914. Here, his potential as an aviator was soon recognised, and a surviving report on him by the chief of the school at that time states that 'Kozakov is an excellent pilot'.

The war with Germany was already several weeks old when Kozakov completed his training as a military pilot at Gatchina on 24 September 1914. However, he had to wait until the end of November to acquire his aeroplane, a Morane-Saulnier Type G. Then, with several other airmen, he was ordered to the front. Leaving to join the 4th KAO on 15 December, they travelled via Warsaw to their unit, which was tasked with providing reconnaissance patrols for the 2nd Siberian and 1st AK (*Armeisky Korpus* – Army Corps) until the end of January 1915.

Kozakov's first flight with the squadron was quite eventful. As he took off on 25 December his engine caught fire and he was forced to land back on the airfield. Thankfully the airframe was saved, but his engine was ruined and he was forced to wait until a replacement could be fitted. Finally, on 6 January 1915, Kozakov took off in his Type G on his first offensive patrol, during which he reconnoitred enemy positions in the region of Skcrnevitzy-Bolilov-Mogely.

The next day brought his first aerial encounter when he chased an enemy aircraft back across the frontline. However, it slipped safely away as Kozakov was unarmed at the time. Perhaps it was this first encounter that made Kozakov recognise the need for aircraft to be armed in some way, as he realised that air combat would become inevitable in the near future – a fact upon which he speculated with other airmen in the officers' mess between duty flights. By the end of January 1915 he had flown seven combat sorties.

The ranking Russian ace of World War 1, Alexander Alexandrovich Kozakov

As noted in chapter one, Peter Nesterov's deliberate collision near Zholkiev on 26 August 1914 had brought down an Austrian aircraft, but it had resulted in his own death, and this convinced Kozakov that such extreme methods of combat were too dangerous to be practical for general employment. At this time the choice of weapons available to pilots for use from their aircraft was limited. Lightweight machine guns, although in widespread service in western Europe, had not made an appearance on the Russian Front, and the heavier guns that were available were suitable only for mounting on larger pusher machines such as the Farman.

Kozakov, now obsessed with the thought of arming his aircraft so that he could bring down an enemy aircraft, considered and dismissed a number of ideas before he eventually conceived a solution that was totally original, and has since become a part of aviation history.

Thinking of a ship, which, closing to board another, would secure itself to its victim with grappling hooks, he decided that 'ships of the air' could use similar devices. His scheme included a small grappling hook (known as a 'cat') fitted with a slab of gun cotton. His plan was to fly above the enemy aircraft, close with it and then, when within range, fire the gun cotton, which would blow the 'cat' into the enemy machine's structure and tear a portion away. Any pilot who was prepared to undertake such an attack really did have to be experienced, courageous and cool-headed. Kozakov, with every intention of testing his device against the enemy, practised with it by tying a rope between a group of trees near the airfield and making low-level runs over it, firing off his 'cat' until he could consistently catch the rope with it.

On 18 March 1915, near the village of Guzow on the right bank of the River Vistula, Kozakov got his chance to use the 'cat' in combat. A German aircraft was carrying out a reconnaissance along the Grodisk-Zhyrardov route, and had dropped three bombs in the rear of a Russian observation balloon position. Kozakov had everything prepared. He made a short takeoff run in Type G MS316 and climbed away to intercept the enemy machine. He found the Albatros and chased it until at last the German aircraft manoeuvred under him and into the desired position. Kozakov later recalled;

'The damned drag anchor got caught and was dangling underneath the enemy aeroplane, so I decided to strike across the uppersurface of the Albatros with the undercarriage of my Morane. Without a moment's

Morane-Saulnier Type G MS162. Kozakov used sister-aircraft MS316 to ram a German Albatros two-seat reconnaissance machine on 18 March 1915, seriously damaging the Type G in the process

thought I pushed the elevator down and collided with the enemy. The undercarriage folded up into my fuselage and then something exploded with a loud whistling noise. Seconds later a piece of the Morane's wing struck my elbow. The Albatros rolled to one side, then folded its wings and dropped like a stone. I had switched off the engine because one blade of the propeller was missing. Having lost my bearings, I began gliding. It was only owing to the shrapnel bursts that I could guess where the Russian front was. At first I went down "parachuting", and even turned upside down, but near the earth I was able to correct my flight and land safely. The impact between the aircraft had been so strong that the Morane's undercarriage was curved inwards under the wings.'

Reports of this encounter disagree as to whether the German crew flying the Albatros perished or survived. German historian von Haenelt lists only one airman as having died on this date, Ltn Bodo Krüger serving as an observer with *Flieger Abteilung* 43, based near Soldau.

Nevertheless, Kozakov was awarded the Gold Sword for Bravery, on 28 July 1915, as a result of this engagement. The accompanying citation stated;

'Although Kozakov did not manage to overthrow the enemy with a special anchor, he brought him down, risking his life with the impact of his aircraft against the uppersurface of the enemy aeroplane. As a result, the reconnaissance and bombing were stopped.'

Kozakov had downed the Albatros despite having to face machine gun fire from the enemy observer. He subsequently made several more patrols with the anchor device fitted to his Type G, but news of this incident had quickly spread amongst German aviation units, and he now found it difficult to approach an enemy aircraft in his Morane. Moreover, he had still been forced to ram his opponent, rather than rely on the anchor alone. Something else was required.

Flown with great success by Kozakov (seen here sitting on its left wheel), Nieuport 10 N222 was unusual in that it was armed with a captured German Maxim IMG 08 7.92 mm Spandau machine gun. The ace flew the aircraft from December 1915 to November 1917, amassing 49 hours and 20 minutes of combat flying time during this period. Kozakov shot down five enemy two-seat reconnaissance aircraft with N222, whilst a sixth possible success went unconfirmed. Note the double-headed eagle emblem of Imperial Russia on the fighter's engine cowling

Kozakov sat in the cockpit of N222. The centre section of the upper wing leading edge was cut away so that the barrel of the fighter's Maxim IMG 08 7.92 mm Spandau machine gun could fire cleanly through the resulting gap, thus missing the propeller. The cut-out was upholstered with aluminium so as to protect the wing from damage when the weapon was fired

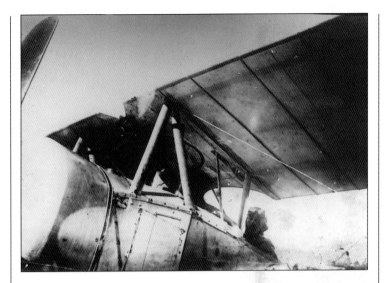

Kozakov continued to fly reconnaissance and bombing missions and, when the opportunity presented itself, he chased enemy aircraft over the frontline too. He quickly earned an enviable reputation for his dedication to duty, aggression in the air and for continually braving enemy gunfire in order to bring back concise and accurate reports. For his courage and dedication Kozakov received several further awards during the course of that year. They included the Orders of St Anne 3rd and 4th Classes with the legend For Bravery and the Order of St Stanislav 3rd Class with Swords and Bow.

On 19 December 1915, having by now gained considerable experience as an operational pilot, Kozakov was appointed commander of the 19th KAO, located near Dvinsk. Soon after his arrival the unit received single-seat Nieuport 10 biplane scout N222, and he immediately 'acquired' it for his own use.

At that stage in the war Russian aviators lacked a reliable system enabling a machine gun to be fired through the propeller arc. Kiev-based aircraft manufacturer V V Jordan had, however, devised a mounting that allowed a gun to be fitted to the top wing at an angle of 24 degrees to the aircraft's axis, thus clearing the propeller when fired. Kozakov quickly had such a mounting fitted to his Nieuport 10. With his aircraft carrying 700 rounds of ammunition, Kozakov at last had a machine capable of effective aerial combat.

Once familiar with N222 and its weaponry, the veteran pilot changed his tactics to the classical direct attack, either from behind or head-on. The gun, being aimed off by 24 degrees, was not ideal, and Kozakov had to rely on his judgement to bring it to bear on his target. Despite these sighting issues, he managed to bring down a pair of Albatros two-seaters with the Nieuport 10. The first of these fell on 14 June 1916 near Lake Drisvyaty, while the second came down on 16 July. The latter machine was engaged during an aerial battle between 12 enemy and 12 Russian aircraft, the German aeroplanes having bombed troops near Dvinsk. Chasing the Albatros towards Lake Drisvyaty, Kozakov eventually managed to force it down near the villages of Skripka and Shaukteli.

A photograph of the cockpit of Kozakov's N222, clearly showing its highly effective machine gun mounting

During the course of 1916, in common with the other major powers engaged in the war, Russia recognised the need to reorganise its aviation service. Until then the fighter detachments of the Russian Army Aviation Service had been few in number, ill equipped and had poor operational coordination. In order to solve these problems, senior officers within the aviation service proposed setting up a BAG. Accordingly, on 9 August the 2nd, 4th and 19th KAOs were combined to form the first such group.

To supplement their original mixed collection of Moranes, Nieuports and Farmans, they acquired a two-seater SPAD A.2 and a Nieuport 10 and 11 Bébé. Pilots had to familiarise themselves with the use of these new machines, as well as developing and practising new group combat tactics. Kozakov played a key role in the establishmnent of the group, and once it had been formed he spent much of his time instructing his men on how the new group would function in combat.

In the third week of August the 1st BAG was ordered to Lutsk to provide cover for an important railway junction nearby that was used to distribute men and supplies to the various fronts. Until then, Austro-German aircraft had met almost no opposition in the air, and had carried out reconnaissance and bombing raids at will. The 1st BAG was tasked with wresting the initiative from them.

Kozakov (third from left) with German PoWs (far left and second from right) from *Flieger Abteiling* 46. The enemy reconnaissance aircraft had been downed by Poruchik Bashinsky and observer Poruchik Guber in a SPAD A.2 on 24 August 1916 after Kozakov had drawn off the machine's escorts

On 24 August the group carried out its first patrol, and Kozakov, in Nieuport 10 N222, accompanied by pilot Poruchik Bashinsky and observer Poruchik Guber in the SPAD A.2, engaged a reconnaissance aircraft and its escort. Kozakov drew off the latter while Bashinsky and Guber attacked the reconnaissance machine (a two-seater from *Flieger Abteilung* 46), bringing it down. Two days later, word reached Lutsk that a formation of seven enemy aircraft was flying near the Kovel-Rozhische railway line. In spite of the enemy's numerical superiority, Kozakov took off alone in N222 and engaged first one and then another of the enemy machines in a running fight that saw his final adversary hit many times. The aircraft was last seen heading off in a westerly direction trailing thick smoke and losing height. This probable victory was never credited to Kozakov, however.

From then until October the group's pilots were regularly engaged in combats and, for the first time during the war, achieved air superiority. The High Command of the Southwestern Front particularly appreciated their work, with military pilot Esaul V M Tkachev, commander of the 11th AD (*Aviatsionnyi Divizion* – Aviation Division), noting that 'The system of squadron air battles yielded excellent results. None of the enemy aircraft could penetrate the airspace above our army, while our own pilots carried out successful reconnaissance – the valiant actions of the glorious group made the enemy forget about Lutsk'.

Under Kozakov's leadership, the aggressiveness and courage of his men compensated in part for the imperfect equipment with which they had to operate. Personally, he took an increasing role in the aerial combats, and during the period from 22 August to 13 September made 12 combat flights totalling 18 hours and 35 minutes, in addition to performing his administrative and training duties. On 7 September his tireless efforts to make the new group successful resulted in his being awarded the Order of St Vladimir 4th Class with Swords and Bow – the foremost class of this honour.

After this hectic period, bad weather in the late autumn curtailed the activities of all of the air forces. However, as soon as the clear frosty weather of early winter came, the Austro-German units resumed their attempts to carry out a reconnaissance of Lutsk.

A photo montage illustrating Kozakov's victory of 8 December over Austrian pilot Kpl Johann Kölbl. The latter, piloting Hansa-Brandenburg C I 27.14, was hit and fell out of the cockpit as the two-seater spiralled earthward. His observer, Oblt Franz Weigl, suffered a wound to his right arm but somehow survived the crash – he can be seen standing alongside Kozakov in the photograph at bottom right

On 8 December a patrol from *Flik* 10 was approaching the town when Kozakov attacked the three machines. Hansa-Brandenburg C I 27.14, crewed by pilot Kpl Johann Kölbl and observer Oblt Franz Weigl, was hit and went tumbling down. During the descent Kölbl, who was already dying, fell out of the cockpit, but Weigl, wounded in the arm, survived the crash landing and became Kozakov's fourth victory. He was also the 1st BAG's guest for a brief while, before being interned as a PoW. For this action, to the great approval of his comrades, Kozakov was given the Order of St George, 4th Class, on 14 January 1917.

The success of the 1st BAG led to three more combat groups being created on other fronts in the East during 1917. However, up to war's end, none gained the esteem and fighting qualities of the 1st BAG. For his efforts, that New Year, Kozakov was officially recommended for the new post of commander of the 1st BAG in preference to the more senior pilot, Polkovnik (Colonel) Yakobashvilli. Kozakov's file stated;

'An outstanding military pilot and officer. By his selfless bravery and resolution he sets an example for his subordinates. Well prepared technically, the internal organisation of his group is perfect. Well prepared and worthy of being appointed Commander of Aviation.'

There were no obstacles to this recommendation, made in February 1917, and so by order number 239 of the Commander of the Rumanian Front, Kozakov was appointed Acting Commander, 1st BAG, on 19 March 1917.

By then the 1st BAG had been ordered to move to the Rumanian Front, but because of the chaos in the railway system at the rear it did not arrive here until the end of March. The group's new area of operation covered the region of Monastryzchesko-Podhaice-Halitch-Brzezany-Svistelniky-Kozovo.

Administrative duties now took up even more of Kozakov's time, but from mid-April he began to fly operational patrols once again. That month he made ten combat flights totalling 12 hours and 45 minutes, and again added to his tally. On 23 April, when flying with pilots drawn from his three squadrons, he attacked an enemy machine, which landed near Brzezany. On 28 April, again with his group, he attacked an aircraft that forced-landed to the west of the village of Sarnky, near Svistelniky-Kuropatniky.

A line-up of 1st BAG fighters at Kovalyuvka airfield in the spring of 1917. They all feature the group's distinctive 'Adam's head' marking on their tails

In May Kozakov flew when he could, managing eight patrols for a total of 14 hours and 20 minutes flying time. During these sorties he scored three more victories, all while flying Nieuport 17 N1910. The first of these came on the 4th whilst he was flying with one of his favourite pilots, Shtabs-Kapitan Pavel Argeev (who the following year would win fame in France flying as Capitane Paul d'Argueff – although a Russian officer, he had travelled to France in 1914, where he received flight training, before returning home in 1916). They attacked an enemy aircraft over Podhaice and forced it to land near the village of Muzchilov. Ltns Witgen and Bode from *Flieger Abteilung* 242 were captured.

On 12 May a Hansa-Brandenburg C I fell victim to Kozakov, landing to the northwest of the village of Kobylniki, and at 0800 hrs on 26 May Kozakov and Argeev, again flying together, brought down a second Hansa-Brandenburg of Kozovo. This aircraft, C I 63.75 from *Flik* 25, was destroyed by its crew, Oblt Paylay and Kpl Kimmel, before they were captured.

This proved to be the final success shared by Kozakov and Argeev, who fled Russia for France following the October 1917 Revolution. Having claimed a number of successes flying with the 19th KAO, he duly served with French fighter unit SPA124 until war's end. Argeev was credited with nine enemy aircraft destroyed between May and October 1918.

In June 1917 a great offensive was launched on the Russian Front, with large formations of supporting troops on the ground. The 1st BAG was involved in the campaign, but Kozakov flew only six missions during this period. Nevertheless, he scored two more victories, the first of these being on 7 June when he attacked one of two enemy machines encountered over Mikulintse while flying Nieuport 10 N222. Rumpler C Ia 4739/16 of *Flieger Abteilung* 24 landed to the east of Podhaice. Its pilot, Fw Bolweg, was slightly wounded in the leg, but his observer, Ltn Deter, had been hit by several of the 50 bullets that had struck the machine.

Members of the 19th KAO pose with German observer Ltn Witgen (fourth from left) of *Flieger Abteilung* 242, who was shot down by Kozakov (fifth from left) and Argeev (third from left) on 4 May 1917

On 14 June Kozakov carried out two combat flights in N1910, the first starting at 0500 hrs. One hour later he attacked a Rumpler near Podhaice, the two-seater falling between the frontline trenches at Lipitsa-Dolno. During the second flight some three hours later Kozakov engaged another Rumpler (from *Flieger Abteilung* 29), but this time things did not go to plan. Following a sharp exchange of fire with the observer, the Russian ace was wounded in the arm. Losing blood, he was forced to disengage and return to base. Praposhchik Leman continued to attack the Rumpler, however, and the two-seater eventually made a forced landing at a Russian airfield. The two pilots from the 19th KAO had hit the aircraft 62 times, wounding the observer in the leg. The pilot escaped unscathed, and both men became PoWs.

Kozakov's considerable experience and illustrious career recommended him to the High Command as eminently suitable for the post of Head of the School of Air Combat at Evpatoria and, on 25 June 1917, the position was made available to him. It was a tempting offer of a high and safe posting in the rear, where he could have lived off his reputation and the adulation of the press and public, instead of enduring the continual stress and risk that came with being a frontline pilot. Kozakov, however, had a very deep sense of loyalty and honour to his country and the men he commanded. On 2 July he replied courteously, but resolutely;

'I ask you not to appoint me to the post of Head of the School of Air Combat. I prefer to remain with the group. Thank you for your offer.'

He would be staying with his men.

The war on the Russian Front was nearing its end. By this time the 1st BAG of the Southwestern Front had become the most famous and advanced formation in the Imperial Military Air Fleet, and its leaders were the highest-scoring pilots, with every intention of increasing their tallies.

On 14 July Kozakov took off in N1910 to undertake a reconnaissance of the Snyatyn-Horodenko-Zaleshchiki-Yagelnitse region. At 1000 hrs he met an enemy Albatros and attacked it together with another pilot, Pod'esaul (Cossack Staff Captain) Shangin. During the fight the German aircraft descended from 2000 m to 200 m (6550 ft to 650 ft), the damaged machine being pursued as far as Obertyn village, northwest of Kolomea, where it made a forced landing in enemy territory.

A Nieuport 17 flown by the 1st BAG during the summer of 1917

A line-up of 1st BAG Nieuports and SPADs near Dunaevtsy in September 1917. The four aircraft on the left, belonging to the group staff, include a Nieuport 10, Nieuport 17 and Kozakov's SPAD VII (the first machines on the left). Fourth from left is Pod'esaul (Cossack Staff Captain) Shangin's Nieuport 17

SPAD VII S1436 at the airfield of the Moscow Aviation Depot in the summer of 1917. The 1st BAG received this machine on 29 August 1917, and Kozakov flew it from 14 October to late November 1917. He claimed his last victory with S1436 on 13 November, when he helped fellow ace Ivan Smirnov force down a German reconnaissance aircraft in enemy territory. This success was never officially credited to Kozakov, however, being solely awarded to Smirnov instead. Later that same month S1436 was captured by Austro-Hungarian troops

Six days later Rotmistr (Captain of Cavalry) Kozakov, who was again flying with Pod'esaul Shangin, attacked an enemy aircraft south of Khotin at 1000 hrs. Their victim was Hansa-Brandenburg C I 64.67 of *Flik* 26, which landed near Dolinyany, in Russian-held territory. The observer, Ltn Franz Slavik, was wounded and taken prisoner, but the pilot, Kpl Trajan Varza, was killed. The aircraft, fitted with Daimler engine wk-nr 2919, was captured in good order.

In August 1917 the 1st BAG moved to Gorodok, from where it was to control part of the Southwestern Front in the Yarmolintsy-Proskurov-Skala-Husyatin-Kutkovtse region. During this month Kozakov made only eight flights, totalling 14 hours and 35 minutes, yet he still managed to claim two more victories. On 16 August he came across an Ago C IV two-seater of *Flieger Abteilung* 24 to the west of Proskurov, and after a short exchange of fire it fell between the villages of Danyuki and Lapkovtsy, 20 km (12 miles) from Proskurov. Both crewmen, pilot Oblt Haushalter and observer Ltn Freinzel, were killed.

Thirteen days later Kozakov scored what was to be his 16th, and last, confirmed victory when he damaged Hansa-Brandenburg C I 269.18 of *Flik* 18 and forced it to crash-land in Russian-held territory. The pilot, Kpl Fritz Weber, and his observer, Oblt Theodor Fischer, became PoWs.

By September 1917 there was very little combat activity on the Russian Front, which was disintegrating as the revolutionary fervour began to grip troops in the frontline. Despite this the 1st BAG continued to operate, and Kozakov flew on seven occasions for a total duration of 14 hours and 20 minutes. One eventful flight occurred on 10 September when, flying alone, he attacked four enemy aircraft near Smotrich. Minutes later

Alexey Shirinkin of the 7th AOI, flying a SPAD VII, entered the fray. He quickly brought down one of the enemy machines near the village of Shidlovtsy, but was then set upon by another German fighter, which caused him to disengage from the battle and make a forced landing. Kozakov, alone once more, remained in the melee and eventually forced his three adversaries to retreat to their own lines.

From 25 September, in a welcome diversion from his frustrations at the front, Kozakov was called upon to sit on the Council of St George. This august body of senior ranking personnel met to determine the merits of the conduct of servicemen recommended for the Cross or Order of St George – Imperial Russia's highest military award. Upon his return to the front 25 days later, Kozakov found it had collapsed completely, thus greatly reducing the 1st BAG's activities. However, he personally was determined to continue to fulfil his duties until ordered otherwise, and during October and November he was in the air for a total of 16 hours and 40 minutes during ten combat missions. He seldom saw the enemy over the lines, however, writing despondently in his despatches 'I didn't come across enemy aircraft'.

In November Kozakov was promoted to the rank of Polkovnik, and on the 21st he was appointed acting commander of the 7th AD and had to leave the 1st BAG. He was also ordered to stop making combat flights over the front by the 'Resolution of the Revolutionary Committee'. Thus, his last flight against the Central Powers came on 20 November when he returned to his airfield without having encountered the enemy. The war in the air against the Austro-Germans was over for Kozakov, but a new and equally stressful period lay ahead. Soon after the order to cease flying was issued, he resigned his command of the 7th AD and requested replacement. This done, he returned to the 1st BAG on 4 December 1917.

By this time all officer ranks and combat rewards had been abolished. Kozakov was no longer a colonel, but he still commanded the group and was held in the utmost esteem by his subordinate pilots. On 9 December at a general meeting of soldiers, and after a long discussion, a secret ballot was held and a new commander for the 1st BAG was elected. The man chosen was former Unter-Officer (NCO) Ul'yan Pavlov, who later rose to high rank in the Soviet Air Force of the 1920s and early 1930s. Three days later, Kozakov, aware that he was now powerless to influence events, turned his duties over to the new man. However, such was the awe in which he was held that all of the soldiers of the 19th KAO took a vote of their own on 17 December and unanimously elected him to stay and lead them.

Kozakov, his character formed by his strict upbringing, and regimented in an attitude of obedience to the Tsar, was a strict disciplinarian. He was courageous in the face of adversity but was also sensitive – a facet of his character which endeared him to those who served under him. He cared about his men and the adversaries whom he had brought down. He always looked after the latter's welfare, supplying them with food and warm clothing, before sending them on to prisons in remote areas of the empire.

Kozakov's own health, however, had suffered terribly during the three years of conflict. There had been the strain of serving in an air force that was inherently inferior to its enemy. He also had to deal with a revolution on the home front where officers were being murdered. Kozakov also bore the burden of leadership. Carrying out the routine running of an operational squadron was a major achievement in itself, as even the most ordinary of supplies were either not delivered or arrived partly plundered! Other ranks would question every decision made by Kozakov, and some of his men had been threatened with death. Indeed, a handful would commit suicide rather than tear off their epaulettes – the symbols of the old regime – as ordered by the 'Resolution of the Revolutionary Committee'. These strains had caused Kozakov to lose weight, thus giving him the gaunt features and haggard eyes seen in later photographs.

On 20 December, by order of the 484th Field Mobile Hospital, he left the front for Kiev to undertake a course of treatment. Travelling as an officer was dangerous, but at this time the Bolsheviks had no intention of harming him. During his stay in Kiev he was approached by the new authorities, asked to help build up the new 'Workers and Peasants Red Air Forces' and had a meeting with the main board of that body. He also had the advantage of learning that the first chief of this new air force was actually a British secret agent who was making every effort to contact the commanding officers of the aviation units so as to build a relationship with them and help them to escape to western Europe if they so wished.

With the landings by the 'Interventionists' in May and June 1918, Kozakov and a number of other illustrious Imperial aviators made their separate ways to Murmansk via the British aviation chief's escape route. On 19 July he was given the rank of major in the Royal Air Force (RAF) and command of the first unit of the newly created 'Slavo-British Aviation Corps', which 34 Russian airmen eventually joined.

For the following year Kozakov led this unit as successfully as he had the 19th KAO and the 1st BAG. Now, however, there was little aerial threat from the enemy, and the only enemy aircraft seen were those brought over by defecting aviators that Kozakov had coaxed from Soviet service (preferably in squadrons, to prevent retribution upon those left behind). His appeal was duly answered by men who had known him in the Imperial Military Air Fleet.

When aloft, Kozakov now spent most of his time bombing and strafing or performing reconnaissance missions. His primary targets were the river barges which formed the enemy's main lines of communications. All of these duties he performed with great elan, impressing his new British colleagues, who decorated Kozakov for his daring low-level flights and the qualities of his command. However, at the end of July 1919 the 'Interventionists' started evacuating and the Slavo-British Corps was to be abolished. Kozakov was offered a post in London, but he refused in order to stay with his men. He was deeply upset and gloomy at the withdrawal of the allies.

On the evening of 1 August 1919 Kozakov ordered his Sopwith Snipe, E6350, to be made ready for a flight from the airfield at Bereznik. Upon taking off from the field he made no attempt to gain height, and his machine flew on at an altitude of only five to ten metres (15-30 ft) for an unusually long period. Then the aircraft's nose lifted as if to make a loop. However, at the highest point of the 'loop' the Snipe lost speed, stalled and fell vertically, nose first, into the ground. Kozakov died before help could reach him, cradled in the arms of the Russian and RAF personnel who had raced to the wreckage of the Snipe. Not yet 31 years of age, he was buried with full military honours in the small chapel in Bereznik.

Ivan Smirnov

Born on 30 January 1895, Ivan Smirnov was the fourth child of a peasant family who occupied a farm not far from Vladimir, east of Moscow. War and voluntary enlistment in the 96th Omsk Infantry Regiment abruptly changed his fate. After a brief spell in a training detachment, Smirnov accompanied the regiment to the Polish city of Lodz. Marching west took two days and the regiment went into battle against German troops, being assigned to the 2nd Army on the Northwest front. Hastily trained Russian soldiers, who had until recently been peasants and labourers, had to face the well armed and trained regular troops of the German army.

Smirnov was awarded a soldier's St George Cross 4th Class (No 89155) by the order of the 2nd Army No 224, dated 13 November 1914, 'for battle reconnaissances from 10 to 24 October'. On 8 December that same year Smirnov was seriously wounded and sent by hospital train to Petrograd. Upon being discharged from hospital, he was given a month's leave to recover with his parents in Vladimir. There, he submitted an official appeal to Grand Duke Alexander Mikhailovich (field inspector-general of the Russian Army Aviation Service) for transfer to flying duties, and he was soon ordered to report to the flying school in Petrograd. Although Smirnov was only a student here from 7 to 25 August 1915, he managed to make his first flight with an instructor on a Caudron primary trainer. Having accumulated three-and-a-half hours of flying time, Smirnov was transferred to the flying school of the Imperial Moscow Society of Aeronautics probably due to overcrowding at the Petrograd flying school.

The primary training at the Moscow school, where Smirnov arrived on 12 October, was conducted on the Farman IV biplane, powered by a 50 hp Gnome engine. His first solo flight was made on this type, and he was the first in his class to successfully complete the primary training course and move on to the so-called 'Farman-battle' (Farman HF XVI).

In the summer of 1916 an order about retraining the most capable cadets on fighters was issued by the Department of the Military Air Fleet. At the beginning of the year the High Command staff had decided to form 12 fighter detachments (one per army), and specially trained pilots were required to reinforce the units' personnel. Smirnov was in the group under instructor Praporshchik Panteleimon Anikin, who taught them how to master fighter tactics using the Morane-Saulnier Type G and Moska MBbis monoplanes. On 28 August Efreitor (Corporal) of the 1st Aviation Park Ivan Smirnov passed his flying examination with the rank of pilot on the Morane-Saulnier Type L monoplane.

Ryadovoi (Soldier) Ivan Smirnov with his first decoration, the Cross of St George 4th Class. This cross was awarded to him by the order of the 2nd Army No 224, dated 13 November 1914, 'for battle reconnaissances from 10 to 24 October'

Aircraft of the 1st BAG await their next patrol on an airfield near Lutsk, on the North Front, in September 1916

It was during this time at the Moscow flying school that Smirnov made friends with Ryadovoi Lipsky, who graduated from the school on Nieuport fighters and was later sent to the 6th AOI. The friends met again a year later, in the autumn of 1917, in the 19th KAO.

After graduating from the Moscow flying school Smirnov was assigned to the newly re-designated 19th KAO in September 1916. This detachment, under the command of Shtabs-Rotmistr Alexander Kozakov, was the best in the Imperial Military Air Fleet. The unit was part of the 1st BAG, which was located not far from Lutsk when Efreitor Ivan Smirnov arrived on 7 September. Shortly after reaching Lutsk, he spotted a tall, lean staff officer with a pomaded moustache, bent over maps. It was Kozakov, who warmly greeted the new pilot. 'Ah! Smirnov! I saw your documents. You have good recommendations. You have joined the best detachment in Russia, where only the best pilots fly. I wish you good luck!'

Smirnov was initially given the two-seat reconnaissance Nieuport 10 to fly, as there were not enough fighters in the group at that point even for the skilled pilots. The 1st BAG was equipped mainly with SPAD A.2 and Nieuport 10 and 11 Bébé biplanes. Smirnov flew with observer Shtabs-Kapitan P A Pentko, who had been attached to the 19th KAO from the 17th Artillery Brigade since May 1916. The latter duly became the young pilot's first frontline instructor and commander.

In September seven pilots of the 19th KAO undertook 33 missions, flying a total of 55 hours. Pentko and Smirnov routinely took off in their two-seat Nieuport alongside single-seat scouts from the group to repulse enemy air raids. On 20 September, flying Nieuport 10 N722, Smirnov and Pentko twice attacked German biplanes undertaking reconnaissance over Lutsk. One of them was pursued up to the trench lines, at which point the enemy crew fired eight rockets as an urgent request for help from anti-aircraft gunners and fighters. The aircraft then descended behind its own lines, whereupon defensive fire forced the Russians to turn back.

With the onset of bad autumn weather, aviation activity on both sides was reduced. The group's pilots flew when the conditions permitted, and on 2 October '15 machines took off for combat, five in the morning and ten in the evening. Ten machines participated in combats', reported the chief of the 1st BAG, Shtabs-Kapitan Zalessky. That month the pilots of

The remains of Aviatik C I C2775/16, which was Smirnov's first victory on 20 December 1916. Flying Nieuport 10 N722, he shared it with his observer, Shtabs-Kapitan Pentko

the 19th KAO sortied 33 times. A further 29 flights were made in November, although Mladshyi Unter-Officer (junior non-commisioned officer) Smirnov made only three of them for a total flying time of six hours and 20 minutes.

The crew of Nieuport 10 N722 gained their first victory on 20 December. That day, Smirnov and Pentko were ordered to attack three German Aviatik C-types flying above Russian positions. Two of the enemy aircraft turned back when the Nieuport approached, but one pilot decided to engage. Attacking at maximum speed, changing course and manoeuvring as much as the Nieuport allowed, Smirnov tried to gain a favourable position from which his observer could get in a good shot. At last he managed to get ahead of his opponent (C-type C2775/16), and an accurate burst from Pentko's Lewis gun finished the fight. The Aviatik spun down into the ground, its pilot apparently having been killed.

That same day fellow future ace Nikolai Kokorin of the 1st BAG's 4th KAO shot down another aeroplane. An archive document describes the two encounters thus;

'Today between 1100 hrs and 1300 hrs the aviation group shot down two aeroplanes near Lutsk. The first was shot down by the volunteer Smirnov and observer Shtabs-Kapitan Pentko and the second by Praporshchik Kokorin in a Monocoque [Morane-Saulnier Type I MS750]. The engagements took place above frontline trenches near Lutsk, and both enemy aeroplanes fell in our positions 1.5 km [one mile] from each other. The enemy airmen (three officers and one corporal) were killed by gunfire in the air. The Albatros aeroplanes were wrecked.'

In fact, Smirnov and Pentko had shot down German Aviatik C I C2775/16, while Kokorin's victim was indeed an Albatros C III.

In the wake of this success Smirnov was recommended for promotion to the officer rank of Praporshchik. As was usually the case in Imperial Russia, however, this recommendation took four months to be passed through different staffs and departments. Finally, on 30 April 1917, it was announced that 'by Order No 506 of the Southwest Front armies, Starshyi Unter-Officer Ivan Smirnov is promoted to the rank of Praporshchik for merit in combat'. This news was published in the orders of the aviation group on 19 May 1917. Pre-empting this award by several months, the CO of the 19th KAO, Shtabs-Rotmistr Kozakov, had used his authority to promote Smirnov to the rank of Starshyi Unter-Officer.

From November 1916 Smirnov began to fly a Morane-Saulnier Type I monoplane, described in Russian reports as the 'Morane-monocoque' or simply 'Monocoque' even though its fuselage was not a monocoque structure.

By late 1916 Grand Duke Alexander Mikhailovich considered the 1st BAG's continued assignment to the Special Army of the Southwest Front to be a waste of precious resources, and he demanded the unit's transfer to the front of the 4th Army. Smirnov's last flights with the 1st BAG in the area of Lutsk, made on 7 and 8 January, consisted of four patrols totalling six hours and 45 minutes.

In January 1917 the 1st BAG was transferred to a southern airfield near Galicia, on the Southwest Front, but for a number of reasons (a shortage of railway cars, transition to European-gauge tracks, the incompetence of railway officials and staff officers, etc.) it took until late March for the unit to finally reach the site. For more than two months the best combat unit of the Imperial Military Air Fleet was inoperative. In a report issued in March 1917, the activities of the 1st BAG were estimated highly by the Command of the Southwest Front;

'At a difficult time the battle aviation group, consisting of the 2nd, 4th and 19th KAOs, arrived at the front. Despite insignificant equipment compared with that of the enemy, by personal strength of spirit the famous battle aviation group, from the first days, forced the conceited enemy to come to his senses, and by winning many valiant air victories, singly and in groups, paralysed his vigorous activity and stopped his unchallenged flights.'

In the same report, the 'selfless bravery and courage of the military pilots of the aviation group', including volunteer Smirnov, was underlined.

On 24 March the 1st BAG arrived at Monastyrzhesko, and on the 27th the pilots resumed combat flying while the Command of the Southwest Front was engaged in finding accommodation and facilities for the group's various fighter detachments. The 4th and 19th KAOs and the 1st BAG's command staff were billeted in Kovalyuvka village, while the 2nd KAO found quarters at Brzeżany station. From archival records it is known that Smirnov made three early flights, patrolling in the area of military positions on 30 and 31 March for a total duration of six hours and five minutes.

On 5 April Smirnov, flying Morane-Saulnier Type I MS740, made four attacking passes on an enemy aircraft over Trostyanets village, firing 120 rounds from a range of just 50 m (160 ft). He pursued the enemy aircraft as far as Sel'tso village, where it disappeared into a cloud. After Smirnov had landed, holes were found in the fuselage and a wing of his Morane. Nine days later Smirnov participated in an action that subsequently saw him recommended for the soldier's Georgian Cross 3rd Class. On that day the pilots of the aviation group flew seven sorties and had four aerial engagements. The details of Smirnov's combat went unrecorded, but it is known that the pilots of the group successfully repulsed several raids by enemy aeroplanes during the second half of the day in the area of Tovstobaby and Yarkhorov.

After shooting down an enemy aircraft on 19 April Smirnov was recommended to receive the soldier's Georgian Cross 2nd Class. News of this award, however, did not reach the group until December 1917 in Order No 398 of the 7th AD;

'Starshyi Unter-Officer Smirnov of the 19th Detachment is awarded the Georgian Cross 2nd Class. On 19 April 1917, having risen to pursue an enemy aeroplane, he attacked and brought it down in the area of the 3rd Caucasian Corps.'

That day, Smirnov had taken off in Type I MS740 and flown a patrol over Kovalyuvka, Zavaluv and Panovitsa, before returning to Kovalyuvka once again. In his report he wrote;

Smirnov and his German prisoner, Alfred Heft, near a Morane-Saulnier Type I at Kovalyuvka airfield in April 1917. The German had been flying the Albatros C-type shot down by the future Russian ace on 19 April. The Type I is possibly MS740, which Smirnov used to down the German reconnaissance aircraft from *Flieger Abteilung (Artillerie) 220*. The victory was shared with 4th KAO pilot Praporshchik Mikhail Malyshev, who was also flying a Type I

'Having risen to pursue the enemy, in the region of Korzhova village I overtook and attacked it at a height of 1200 m [4000 ft], firing 100 bullets. I then flew away to correct a stoppage of the machine gun, before attacking it once again. After the second attack the enemy aeroplane descended in the region west of Gorozhanki village.'

Eyewitnesses of this combat and the landing of the German aeroplane were pilot Praporshchik Krisanov and his gunner, soldier Yakutin, who were flying a Nieuport 10 near Zavaluv. The other participant in the engagement was 4th KAO pilot Praporshchik Mikhail Malyshev, who reported;

'Flying a Monocoque, I caught up with the enemy aeroplane at a height of 1300 m [4250 ft] and fired a burst of 30 cartridges, but there was a misfire'.

Malyshev then broke off his pursuit, and watched another Monocoque from the 19th KAO attack the enemy aeroplane. He continued;

'I again flew nearer to the enemy and fired a short burst. At last another Monocoque attacked the enemy from the right, after which a white jet of steam appeared and the enemy aeroplane landed in a hollow on a road. It turned on landing, but did not flip over. A German jumped out and set fire to the right wing.'

Malyshev was therefore first to attack the Albatros C-type, but he was unable to finish it off owing to machine gun failure. Smirnov completed the job. Only the burned aeroplane's six-cylinder 220 hp Mercedes engine, wk-nr 210, remained as a trophy. His victims, pilot Alfred Heft and an unnamed officer observer of *Flieger Abteilung (Artillerie) 220*, were taken prisoner, the latter having been wounded in the leg. Such German squadrons were organised exclusively for artillery spotting. In memory of this event Smirnov was photographed near his Type I with the captive German pilot.

At 0900 hrs on 3 May Podporuchik (Second Lieutenant) Zhabrov of the 2nd KAO and Praporshchik Smirnov of the 19th KAO engaged a Fokker monoplane fighter in combat north of Bol'shovtse. Following the encounter the German pilot descended abruptly in his own territory, and after landing Smirnov and Zhabrov found bullet holes in their aircraft.

This photograph of Smirnov was taken when he visited an airfield of the 7th AOI during the spring of 1917. For a long time the French-built Nieuport 21 in this shot (camouflaged in Western Front dark brown and greyish green) from Smirnov's album was identified by researchers as belonging to the 19th KAO. However, according to archive documents, N1514 and Nieuport 11 N1232 in the background, belonged to the 7th AOI, which, like the 1st BAG, was included in the 7th AD. Moreover, their airfields were not far from one another on the Southwest Front

Eight days later Praporshchik Smirnov and Unter-Officer Serikov took off at 0900 hrs to escort a reconnaissance aeroplane of the 1st Artillery Aviation Detachment that was to photograph enemy positions. Serikov engaged an enemy aircraft near Shumlyany, forcing the German machine to flee.

By 20 May Praporshchik Smirnov had flown 42 sorties with a total duration of 70 hours and 20 minutes. His dedication to service saw him recommended for promotion to a military pilot rank in recognition of his accomplishments. The following day Smirnov was given a month's leave as his award, and he returned to the 19th KAO on 20 June.

By then the unit had relocated to an airfield near Kovalyuvka village, and Smirnov soon resumed combat flying. On 22 June he took off in a Type I on a patrol with Praporshchik Shaitanov, who was flying a Nieuport 21. As they neared Shibalin the Russian pilots spotted two enemy Fokker monoplanes, but they failed to attack them as their aircraft were too slow to overhaul the German machines. Smirnov made a second flight that day, but he did not encounter any enemy machines. The next day Smirnov used a Type I to escort the crew of a Farman who were photographing enemy positions. He wrote;

'Southwest of Brzezhany I noticed an enemy fighter that wanted to attack the photographing Farman. Having spotted me, he tried to join battle, but after several unsuccessful attempts my opponent flew away to Rogatin. The Farman fulfilled the task, and I continued to patrol northwest to Podhaice, not far from our balloons.'

From 22 June Smirnov flew Nieuport 17 N2522, but he did not meet any opponents on his first patrol with the French biplane. The following day he took off to pursue enemy aeroplanes, but the engine in his fighter stopped shortly after takeoff and he was forced to glide down. Before landing the aeroplane side-slipped, and when it touched down the Nieuport overturned. Although the fighter was damaged, Smirnov was lucky to sustain only slight injuries. On 27 and 28 June Smirnov completed more uneventful patrols. Interestingly, on the latter date he escorted a British reconnaissance machine belonging to Maj Valentine's detachment in the Slobodka-Cheremkhuv region.

On 2 July, by the order of Southwest Front staff, the 1st BAG was transferred to the 8th Army. Two days later the pilots flew patrols along the southern outskirts of Stanislav. By then the June offensive of the Russian armies, started on the initiative of the Provisional Government, had met with failure. At first the troops of the 8th Army had managed to break through the enemy defences south to Stanislav, but on 6 July German forces made a powerful counter-stroke and the 8th Army troops offered almost no resistance, abandoning their positions en masse.

The previous day Smirnov reported;

'While flying a Nieuport 17 in the region of Bol'shovtse I met an enemy aeroplane, attacked it and forced it to go away and descend on the German side of the lines. In the region of Svistel'niki I met an enemy aeroplane, which I attacked three times. After the last attack the enemy aeroplane fled back across the frontline.'

On 8 July Smirnov 'pursued an enemy aeroplane at a height of 4000 m [13,000 ft]. The enemy disappeared in clouds and was not found'.

 (text continues on page 42)

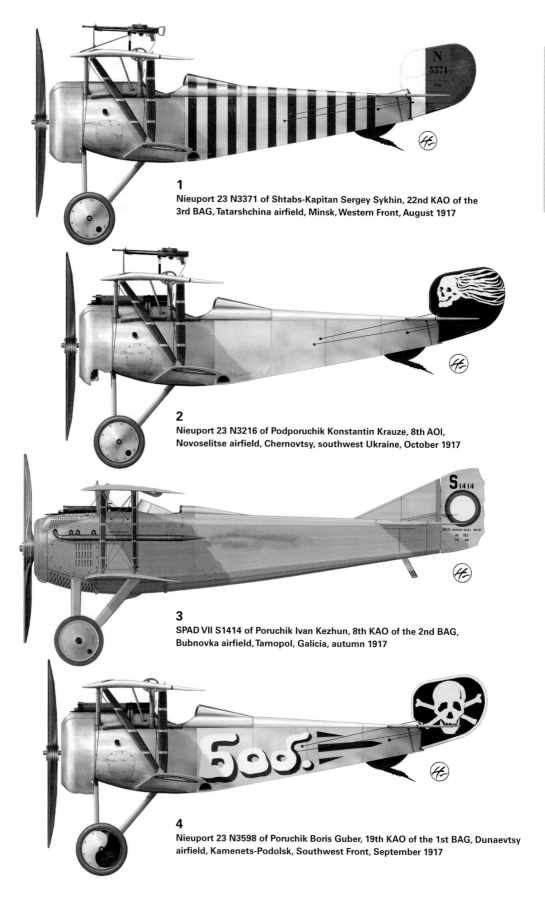

1
Nieuport 23 N3371 of Shtabs-Kapitan Sergey Sykhin, 22nd KAO of the 3rd BAG, Tatarshchina airfield, Minsk, Western Front, August 1917

2
Nieuport 23 N3216 of Podporuchik Konstantin Krauze, 8th AOI, Novoselitse airfield, Chernovtsy, southwest Ukraine, October 1917

3
SPAD VII S1414 of Poruchik Ivan Kezhun, 8th KAO of the 2nd BAG, Bubnovka airfield, Tarnopol, Galicia, autumn 1917

4
Nieuport 23 N3598 of Poruchik Boris Guber, 19th KAO of the 1st BAG, Dunaevtsy airfield, Kamenets-Podolsk, Southwest Front, September 1917

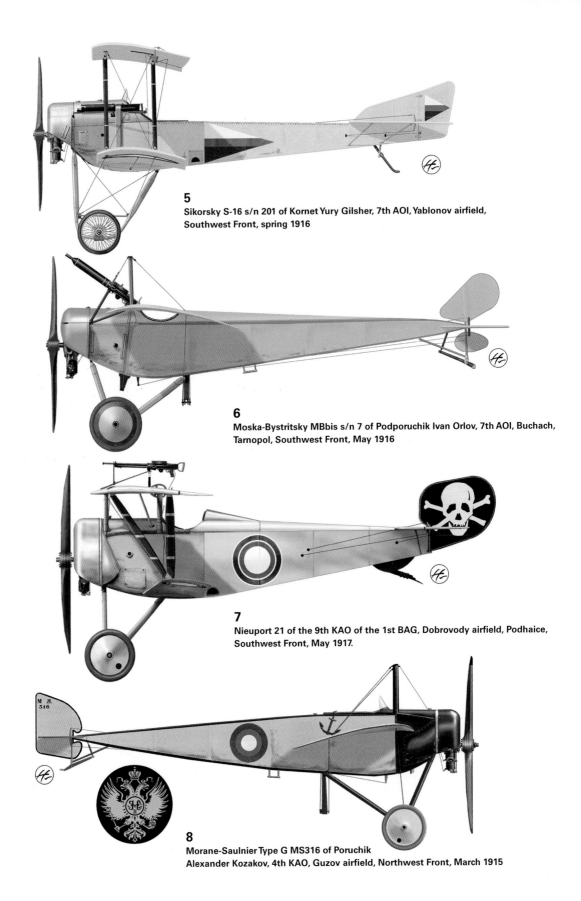

5
Sikorsky S-16 s/n 201 of Kornet Yury Gilsher, 7th AOI, Yablonov airfield, Southwest Front, spring 1916

6
Moska-Bystritsky MBbis s/n 7 of Podporuchik Ivan Orlov, 7th AOI, Buchach, Tarnopol, Southwest Front, May 1916

7
Nieuport 21 of the 9th KAO of the 1st BAG, Dobrovody airfield, Podhaice, Southwest Front, May 1917.

8
Morane-Saulnier Type G MS316 of Poruchik Alexander Kozakov, 4th KAO, Guzov airfield, Northwest Front, March 1915

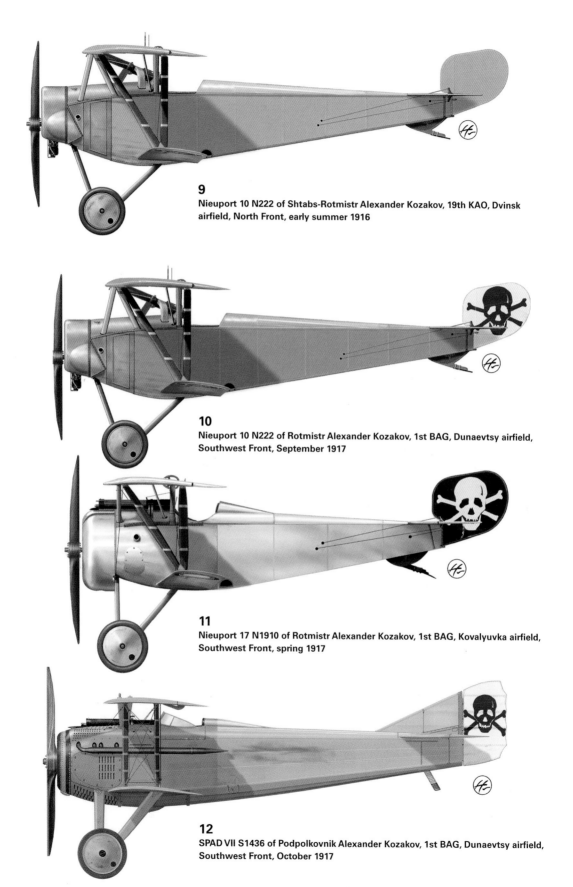

9
Nieuport 10 N222 of Shtabs-Rotmistr Alexander Kozakov, 19th KAO, Dvinsk
airfield, North Front, early summer 1916

10
Nieuport 10 N222 of Rotmistr Alexander Kozakov, 1st BAG, Dunaevtsy airfield,
Southwest Front, September 1917

11
Nieuport 17 N1910 of Rotmistr Alexander Kozakov, 1st BAG, Kovalyuvka airfield,
Southwest Front, spring 1917

12
SPAD VII S1436 of Podpolkovnik Alexander Kozakov, 1st BAG, Dunaevtsy airfield,
Southwest Front, October 1917

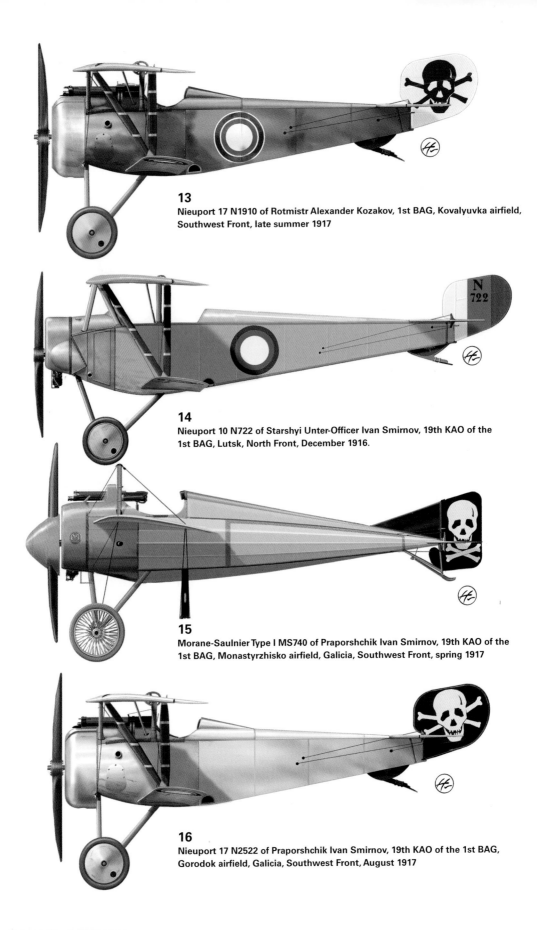

13
Nieuport 17 N1910 of Rotmistr Alexander Kozakov, 1st BAG, Kovalyuvka airfield, Southwest Front, late summer 1917

14
Nieuport 10 N722 of Starshyi Unter-Officer Ivan Smirnov, 19th KAO of the 1st BAG, Lutsk, North Front, December 1916.

15
Morane-Saulnier Type I MS740 of Praporshchik Ivan Smirnov, 19th KAO of the 1st BAG, Monastyrzhisko airfield, Galicia, Southwest Front, spring 1917

16
Nieuport 17 N2522 of Praporshchik Ivan Smirnov, 19th KAO of the 1st BAG, Gorodok airfield, Galicia, Southwest Front, August 1917

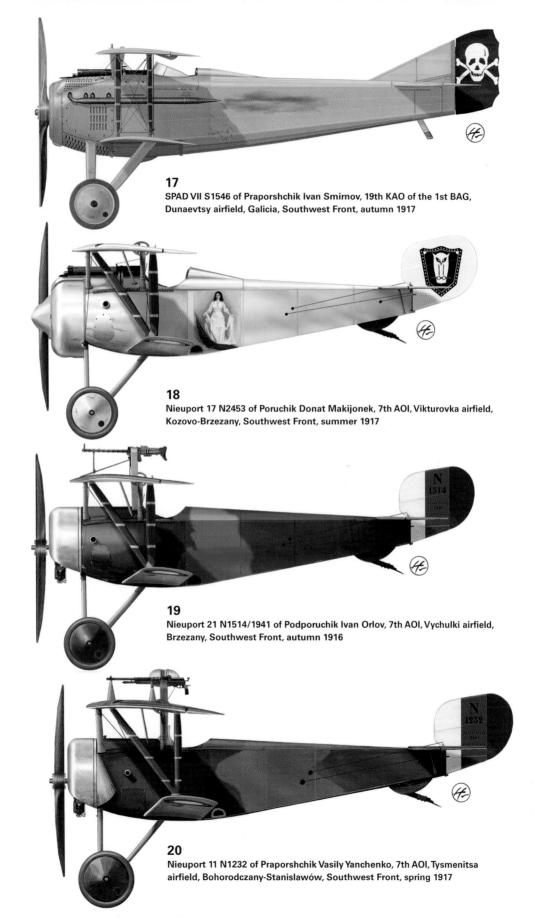

17
SPAD VII S1546 of Praporshchik Ivan Smirnov, 19th KAO of the 1st BAG,
Dunaevtsy airfield, Galicia, Southwest Front, autumn 1917

18
Nieuport 17 N2453 of Poruchik Donat Makijonek, 7th AOI, Vikturovka airfield,
Kozovo-Brzezany, Southwest Front, summer 1917

19
Nieuport 21 N1514/1941 of Podporuchik Ivan Orlov, 7th AOI, Vychulki airfield,
Brzezany, Southwest Front, autumn 1916

20
Nieuport 11 N1232 of Praporshchik Vasily Yanchenko, 7th AOI, Tysmenitsa
airfield, Bohorodczany-Stanislawów, Southwest Front, spring 1917

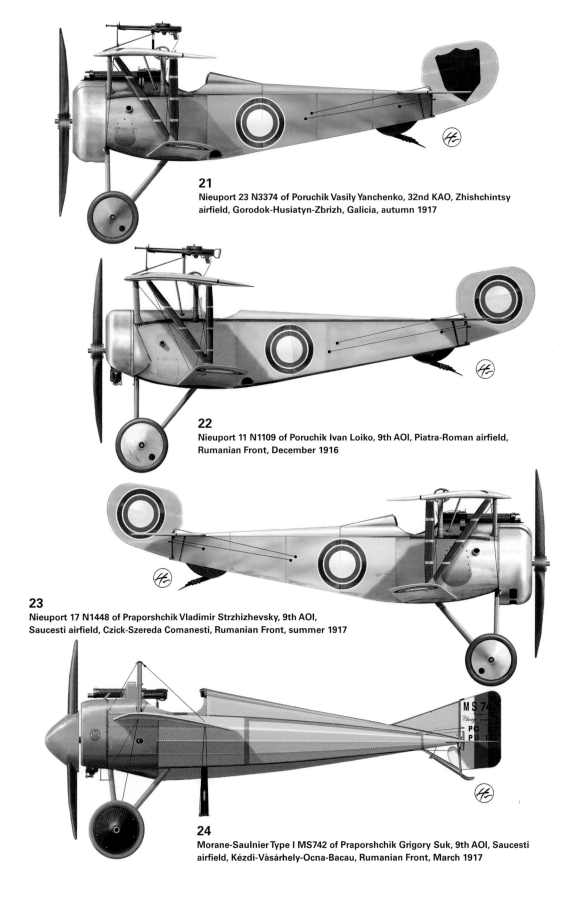

21
Nieuport 23 N3374 of Poruchik Vasily Yanchenko, 32nd KAO, Zhishchintsy
airfield, Gorodok-Husiatyn-Zbrizh, Galicia, autumn 1917

22
Nieuport 11 N1109 of Poruchik Ivan Loiko, 9th AOI, Piatra-Roman airfield,
Rumanian Front, December 1916

23
Nieuport 17 N1448 of Praporshchik Vladimir Strzhizhevsky, 9th AOI,
Saucesti airfield, Czick-Szereda Comanesti, Rumanian Front, summer 1917

24
Morane-Saulnier Type I MS742 of Praporshchik Grigory Suk, 9th AOI, Saucesti
airfield, Kézdi-Vàsárhely-Ocna-Bacau, Rumanian Front, March 1917

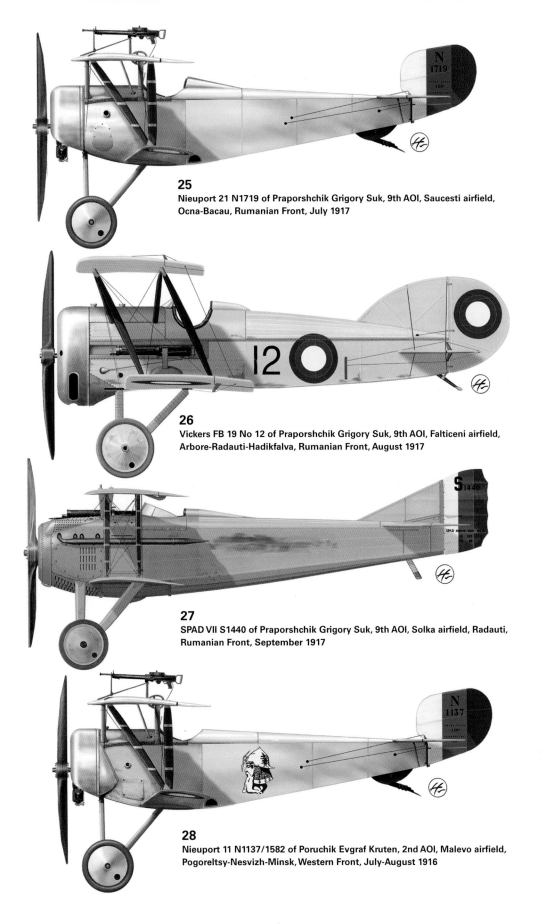

25
Nieuport 21 N1719 of Praporshchik Grigory Suk, 9th AOI, Saucesti airfield,
Ocna-Bacau, Rumanian Front, July 1917

26
Vickers FB 19 No 12 of Praporshchik Grigory Suk, 9th AOI, Falticeni airfield,
Arbore-Radauti-Hadikfalva, Rumanian Front, August 1917

27
SPAD VII S1440 of Praporshchik Grigory Suk, 9th AOI, Solka airfield, Radauti,
Rumanian Front, September 1917

28
Nieuport 11 N1137/1582 of Poruchik Evgraf Kruten, 2nd AOI, Malevo airfield,
Pogoreltsy-Nesvizh-Minsk, Western Front, July-August 1916

17
SPAD VII S1546 of Praporshchik Ivan Smirnov, 19th KAO of the 1st BAG,
Dunaevtsy airfield, Galicia, Southwest Front, autumn 1917

19
Nieuport 21 N1514/1941 of Podporuchik Ivan Orlov, 7th AOI, Vychulki airfield,
Brzezany, Southwest Front, autumn 1916

20
Nieuport 11 N1232 of Praporshchik Vasily Yanchenko, 7th AOI, Tysmenitsa
airfield, Bohorodczany-Stanislawów, Southwest Front, spring 1917

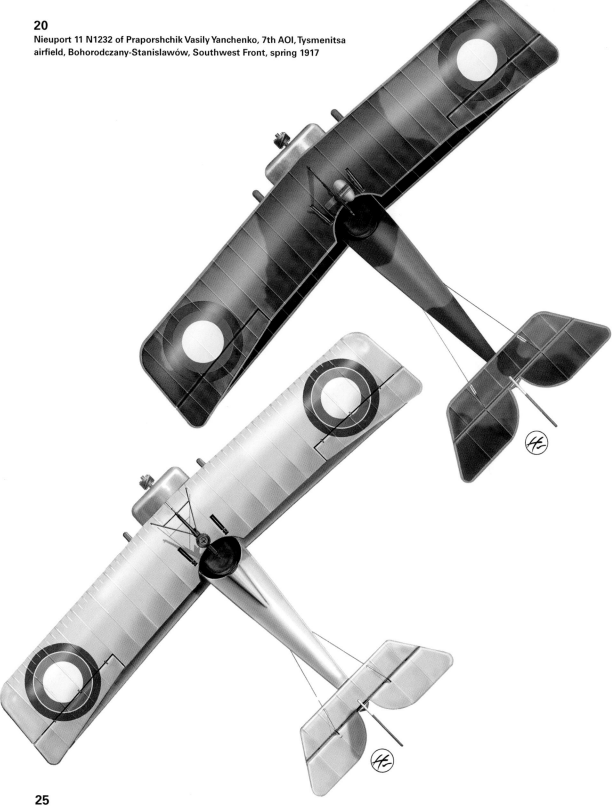

25
Nieuport 21 N1719 of *Praporshchik* Grigory Suk, 9th AOI, Saucesti airfield,
Ocna-Bacau, Rumanian Front, July 1917

The 1st BAG did not stay in Stanislav for long, transferring to Kolomea on 10 July and later to Khotin and Larga, ahead of the retreating troops. On 13 July Smirnov escorted a reconnaissance Farman tasked with flying over Kolomea-Zaleshchiki-Chortkov-Snyatyn. Later that same day, flying a Nieuport 17, he repeatedly took off to undertake additional reconnaissance in this region.

On 17 July, flying with Praposhchik Leman, Smirnov reconnoitred Zaleshchiki. Whilst over the town they attacked an enemy aeroplane, which descended to the rear of the German lines in the direction of Buchach. On 20 July, during a reconnaissance flight at a height of 1500 m (5000 ft) east of Mel'nitse, the engine of Smirnov's Nieuport stopped and he had to glide down, making a successful landing near the village of Georgievtsy. The next day Smirnov made two more patrols, but 'did not meet enemy aeroplanes'. In July Praporshchik Smirnov had completed a total of 11 combat flights and six flights to new bases.

In the 1st BAG's diary on 28 July it was recorded that 'By the Order No 599 of the Supreme Commander-in-Chief dated 9 July 1917, pilot of the 19th KAO Praporshchik Smirnov was awarded the title of "military pilot" for merit in combats with the enemy'. On 31 July the 1st BAG was returned to the control of the 7th Army, the group settling down at airfields in the region of Gorodok.

Smirnov's combat activity in August 1917 was quite intensive, the pilot flying 27 sorties (mostly in Nieuport 17 N2522) for a total flying time of 56 hours – he was the first pilot in the 19th KAO to attain such high figures. On 1 August Poruchik Guber and Praporshchiks Smirnov and Leman took off to patrol in the region of Khotin-Skala-Borshchuv-Germanyuvka, but encountered no enemy aircraft. On their way back Smirnov descended, and at a height of 800 m (2600 ft) attacked an enemy aircraft, which then landed. This victory was not taken into consideration, however, because the combat took place over enemy territory.

During a patrol on 3 August Smirnov 'attacked an enemy aeroplane in the area of Skalat and pursued it with Leman for 24 km [15 miles] into the enemy's rear, having forced it down from a height of 3000 m [9800 ft] to 800 m [260ft]. At Khotin I attacked another aeroplane, which escaped by descending in the direction of Mel'nitse. At Mel'nitse I fired at an enemy balloon, which descended to the ground'.

An entry in the 1st BAG's diary in November 1917 includes a brief list of aeroplanes shot down by different pilots of the group since the date it was established. Smirnov's third victory is dated 3 August. Five days later Smirnov and Poruchik Guber, having noticed shrapnel bursts and an enemy aeroplane east of Husiatyn, attacked the latter machine, which descended in the direction of the enemy's rear lines to avoid a fight.

On 10 August the same two pilots, while patrolling over Husiatyn and Horodnytsia, had 'six consecutive fights with different enemy aeroplanes. We initially attacked a machine at 2000 hrs, chasing it down to a height of less than 400 m [1300 ft]. It was observed that, just as the aeroplane crossed a grove, it descended near Ludvipol village, west of Horodnytsia. One of the crew got out of the aeroplane, but the other remained there, either badly wounded or killed. Evidently, the radiator and engine were pierced, as a large jet of steam was seen'. Guber reported that the aircraft turned over, and that he 'fired at people who approached it from a height of 400 m'. According to another report about this combat, Smirnov and Guber 'forced the enemy aeroplane to descend at Ludvipol village, and when the machine turned over it was fired upon by our pilots from a height of 400 m'.

During two patrol flights on 11 August 'enemy aeroplanes were not found'. The following day the commander of the 7th Army took off in a Voisin biplane on a reconnaissance mission, as he wanted to see the position of German forces for himself. He was escorted by a flight of three fighters from the 19th KAO, the aircraft being flown by Praporshchiks Smirnov and Leman and Poruchik Guber. Again, no enemy aircraft were encountered.

On 15 August Smirnov 'met an enemy aeroplane west of Gorodok and joined battle, which lasted until all my cartridges were spent'. The following day 'north of Skala at 1915 hrs, I attacked two enemy aeroplanes. One of them, a fighter, abruptly went down, it was impossible to observe its fall. The other, a reconnaissance machine, dived towards the ground and, just before reaching the ground, levelled out and flew away to its base'.

On both 20 and 30 August Smirnov escorted Sikorsky Il'ya Mouromets four-engined bombers, reporting 'no enemy aeroplanes approached the air ships'. Between these two dates, on 25 August, he reported 'in the region of Husiatyn I attacked an enemy aeroplane that flew from Gorodok. Emitting smoke, the enemy machine descended abruptly. For the remaining time no enemy was met'. Unfortunately, no other independent confirmation for this victory has yet come to light, the enemy aeroplane possibly coming down in German-held territory. During Smirnov's remaining August flights he either 'did not meet enemy aeroplanes' or they avoided action.

Aside from escorting the Mouromets bombers on 30 August, Smirnov subsequently undertook a patrol with Praporshchik Shaitanov. The former reported that 'in the Husiatyn region we attacked two enemy fighters, one of which was forced to descend to 400 metres', but Smirnov was then compelled to break off as he was short of fuel. The enemy aeroplane turned for base, pursued by Shaitanov. According to other records, the latter shot it down – the fighter's demise was credited to both pilots.

During four patrols mounted in early September Smirnov either did not meet enemy aircraft or they retreated when he approached. Finally, on the 11th, while flying SPAD VII S1546 (which he would

An unnamed German pilot from *Flieger Abteilung* 24 stands alongside Smirnov in front of the latter's Nieuport 17 N2522 at Dunaevtsy airfield on the Southwest Front. The Russian ace had actually used his SPAD VII S1546 to down his opponent's Albatros C X on 11 September 1917 . . .

. . . which is seen here being examined by Russian troops after it was force-landed near Balin. The aircraft's kadett pilot was unhurt during the engagement, but his leutnant observer suffered from a slight head wound. This aircraft, fitted with a 260 hp Mercedes engine, represented Smirnov's sixth confirmed victory

Smirnov, on the left, with the pilot from the downed Albatros C X from *Flieger Abteilung* **24**

use to claim all of his subsequent victories) in the region of Balin, Smirnov shot down an Albatros C X fitted with a 260 hp Mercedes engine. The aircraft successfully forced landed and was immediately claimed as an almost undamaged trophy by the Russians. Its German crew, from *Flieger Abteilung* 24, were captured, the kadett pilot being unhurt and his leutnant observer suffering from a slight head wound. This aircraft represented Smirnov's sixth confirmed victory. In his report of this combat he wrote;

'Having taken off to pursue an enemy aeroplane in the region of Balin, I overtook it and after a short fight shot it down. The enemy aeroplane descended and partly turned over to the west of Balin. The observer was slightly wounded in the head and the pilot was safe and taken into captivity. I received a hole in a wing.'

Smirnov was photographed standing near the Albatros with the captive pilot.

During his second flight on 20 September Smirnov 'attacked an enemy aeroplane at 1700 hrs to the north of Husiatyn and pursued it up to a height of 1000 m [3300 ft] over enemy territory. Not far from the small town of Krasne, I then met about ten enemy aeroplanes. When my machine gun became jammed I could only manoeuvre with them'. The next day a flight of three machines from the 19th KAO, comprising Smirnov in a SPAD VII and Poruchik Guber and Podporuchik Zhabrov in Nieuport 23s, patrolled in the region of Husiatyn-Skala-Grzhimaluv. Smirnov subsequently reported, 'south of Skala I attacked an enemy aeroplane and fired about 90 rounds at it, then my machine gun jammed. At the very same moment my petrol tank was pierced. Returned safely to airfield'.

Despite the weak activity of the Russian armies on the ground in October 1917, the war in the air continued apace. On the 2nd a flight of three aeroplanes from the 19th KAO, flown by Smirnov, Zhabrov and Shaitanov, took off on patrol. In the region of Ratkovtsy Smirnov attacked an enemy aeroplane;

'Having noticed me, it turned back sharply. While attacking I fired about 150 rounds at it. Having pursued it over our trenches south of Grzhimalov at a height of 800 m [2600 ft], I was compelled to stop the pursuit for I could not free the jammed machine gun.'

During subsequent patrols on 3, 5 and 10 October Smirnov did not meet any enemy aircraft. According to the 1st BAG's diary of flights, Smirnov did not fly on the 11th, but in the division's list his next victory was, almost certainly erroneously, credited to him on that date! On 14 October the 1st BAG was transferred from Kovalyuvka to Dunaevtsy – Smirnov flew there the next day. On 17 October he 'attacked an enemy aeroplane in the region southeast of Grzhimalov at 1600 hrs and pursued it to the trenches, having descended with it to a height of 600 m [2000 ft].

In the region of Skala at about 1700 hrs I attacked two enemy fighters and conducted an inconclusive 20-minute fight over enemy territory'.

On 28 October Praporshchik Smirnov, flying his SPAD VII, and Mladshy Unter-Officer Lipsky in a Nieuport 23 took off on a patrol. South of Husiatyn they attacked three Austrian Hansa-Brandenburg C I biplanes, which Smirnov mistook for German aircraft. He later recalled;

'Information reached us about two enemy aeroplanes. Lipsky and I immediately started the engines of our fighters, but when his failed I decided to take off alone. I was 200 m [650 ft] above the enemy aircraft, which were performing a reconnaissance mission. Once I had closed on one of the German aeroplanes I opened fire. I quickly saw that I had hit it, despite having fired from the maximum permissible range. The German machine began to glide like a leaf, then suddenly burst into flames, leaving a long trail of oily black smoke. I switched my attention to the other aeroplane, but when I attacked it my machine gun jammed. I could only circle near it.

'Suddenly I noticed Lipsky. I continued to distract the German's attention, flying around him so that Lipsky could approach unobserved. Before the enemy realised what had happened, Lipsky dived, firing a vortex of bullets into him. The German quickly caught fire and followed his comrade downwards.'

Another view of this encounter was given in the official report tabled by Lipsky and Smirnov. The first attack by the latter pilot was made at 'about 1700 hrs in the region of Zelenaya Sloboda village. I attacked an enemy aeroplane of Hansa-Brandenburg type, which after my several attacks caught fire and fell in our territory, east of Zelenaya Sloboda village. At the same moment I noticed another enemy and attacked him, but after 50-60 shots my machine gun jammed and I stopped the pursuit. At a height of 500-600 m, the pursuit was continued by volunteer Lipsky'.

Lipsky reported;

'In the region of Zelenaya Sloboda, flying at a height of 5300 m [17,400 ft], I noticed two enemy aeroplanes at a height of 1000 m [3300 ft]. Having made a wide turn, I headed for the nearest one. At that time I noticed our SPAD, which attacked the other aeroplane. After the second attack the enemy machine caught fire. Having changed direction for the second time, I began to pursue the other aeroplane simultaneously with the SPAD. Soon the SPAD flew away, while I, pursuing the enemy, fired a burst. Pursuing him down to a height of 500 m, I saw the aeroplane land and turn over. As I flew above the overturned aircraft I saw shells burst near it. The second aeroplane was shot down over Zbruch, falling on enemy wire entanglements near Zelena village and being destroyed by our artillery. A third Hansa-Brandenburg flew off to the rear, this aeroplane having been significantly lower than the other two.'

According to information in the Austrian archives, Hansa-Brandenburg C I 269.08, shot down by Smirnov, 'fell in flames on enemy territory south of Zelenaya Sloboda village'. It belonged to *Flik* 9, and pilot Kpl Josef Ryba and observer Ltn Josef Barcal were killed. It was the seventh aeroplane shot down by Smirnov. The second machine was credited to both Lipsky (his first victory) and Smirnov.

Command rewarded Smirnov and his fellow fighter pilots for their recent successes, declaring that 'by the Order of the 7th Army by the recommendation of the Georgian Duma (special council) of 31 October 1917, the Order of St George 4th Class is awarded to Praporshchiks Leman, Navrotsky and Smirnov'. Unfortunately, it is not clear for which of the enemy aeroplanes Praporshchik Smirnov was awarded this most prestigious officer's order.

The 1st BAG mounted few patrols in November 1917 because of adverse weather conditions, the group's diary frequently recording that 'owing to bad weather there were no flights'. When the weather permitted, the unit made 10-15 combat flights per day. One such day was 10 November, as the 1st BAG combat diary noted;

'At 1530 hrs in the region of the villages at Lany-Koruna-Votin, Praporshchik Smirnov attacked and shot down a German aeroplane, which fell south of Letovo village. The aeroplane was wrecked and the soldier-pilot and officer-observer perished. The enemy aeroplane was a single-strutter type like a Nieuport, its surfaces being covered with plywood and the observer's position being fitted with a rear-firing machine gun. The aeroplane was wrecked, which meant that it was not possible to save any documents.'

It is quite possible that Smirnov had shot down Lloyd C V 46.22 of *Flik* 18 (pilot Zgf Leopold Marasz, observer Oblt Karl Ulrich) for his ninth victory.

Reporting on Smirnov's successes on 28 October and 10 November, Podpolkovnik Kozakov, commander of the 1st BAG, wrote;

'In both cases the aeroplanes were completely smashed – the crew were killed during the descent, then undressed and robbed where they fell. All documents disappeared.'

The Commander-in-Chief of the Military Air Fleet of democratic Russia, Polkovnik Tkachev, sent a telegram to the 1st BAG on 14 November;

'The ninth victory of Praporshchik Smirnov in the days of coming ruin and fatal danger to our long-suffering native land assures us that our valiant pilots will execute their duty up to the end, and will stay at their onerous but famous posts, adding new laurels to a wreath of glory for our native aircraft.'

In the Skalat region at 1300 hrs on 13 November Podpolkovnik Kozakov and Praporshchik Smirnov attacked a German biplane, which descended steeply to 400 m (1300 ft) over the village of Konstantinovka, in enemy-held territory. They then attacked two more German two-seat reconnaissance aeroplanes at 1400 hrs south of Skala, one of which landed in enemy territory near Germanyuvka. This machine gave Smirnov his tenth, and final, victory.

He soon received his last decoration, Order No 398 of the 7th AD being published in the diary of the 1st BAG on 24 December 1917. It stated that 'Military pilot Praporshchik Smirnov of the 19th KAO is awarded the soldier's St George Cross 1st Class for feats of arms from 10 August to 18 September, and for shooting down two enemy aeroplanes'. This was an unusual award, as Smirnov was only issued with it owing to the Provisional Government's decision, on 24 June 1917, to 'reward officers with the soldier's St George Cross'. The awarding of this decoration to officers for feats of personal courage was approved by votes cast by soldiers of the relevant unit concerned, with their decision being confirmed by the commander of the division to which the unit was assigned.

When the war ended, the disorganisation of the army and Bolshevist propaganda also affected the 1st BAG. On 5 December Podpolkovnik Kozakov, temporarily leading the 7th AD, which included his aviation group, was compelled to sign an order stopping all flights 'in accordance with the decision of the Revolutionary Military Committee of the 7th AD'. This order was also signed by soldier Ryzhkov, the commissar at the department of the 7th AD. After that the endless meetings and elections of soldiers' committees began at division, group and detachment level.

On 9 December pilot-soldier Ivan Pavlov was elected commander of the group, and Kozakov handed over all affairs to him. By that time the 1st BAG had practically ceased to exist as a combat unit. Although Kozakov was unanimously elected commander of the Aviation Detachment at a general meeting of the soldiers of the 19th KAO on 17 December, he could do nothing in the prevailing revolutionary chaos, and three days later he left for medical treatment.

Smirnov and his friends Lipsky and Silakov could delay their departure no longer, and having seized an automobile they left in the night for Kamenets-Podolsk. An entry in the diary of the 1st BAG for 20 January 1918 reads as follows;

'Military pilot Praporshchik Smirnov and observer Silakov of the 19th KAO fled from the group at night on 14 December 1917, and up to now they have not come back to be struck off the lists of missing personnel and are to be considered deserters.'

Having arrived in Kamenets-Podolsk, the trio clandestinely boarded a train leaving the frontlines. For almost a month they travelled all over the country, from one city to another, hiding and subjecting themselves to danger on a near-daily basis. They passed through Siberia and arrived in Vladivostok, where the Bolsheviks' power had not yet reached. There, they visited the consulates of the USA and France and tried to join the aviation services of these nations, but met with refusals. The British consul advised them not to remain in Russia at such a disturbing time, but to leave for England, where they could enlist in the Royal Flying Corps (RFC). With the help of a friend, Smirnov managed to obtain the foreign passport of a citizen of the former Russian Empire, which permitted his passage to distant Great Britain.

When Smirnov and Lipsky boarded a steamship they could not have imagined that their journey would last nine months. During that time they exchanged a comfortable cabin for the stoke hold, and in Singapore they ended up in a camp for PoWs, from which they successfully escaped. Shanghai, Hong Kong, Saigon and Singapore remained in their memories for the intolerable tropical heat. Then came Rangoon, Colombo, Aden and Suez, where Smirnov and Lipsky served for some time in a British squadron, taking to the air in an Airco DH 9 for the first time in many months. From there they sailed on to Port Said and Alexandria, and their travels finally ended in the English port of Plymouth, in Devon.

Initially, the War Ministry in London denied their application to serve in the RAF, but the Russian pilots persisted and, with the help of Air Vice-Marshal Sefton Brancker (then Controller-General of Personnel on the Air Council), they were ordered to report to the Central Flying School (CFS) at Upavon in Wiltshire. There, they underwent instruction on Avro 504Ks, Bristol F 2B Fighters and RAF SE 5as, and renewed their aerobatic skills. Upon graduating from the CFS they received their long-desired pilots' wings.

By then, however, World War 1 had ended. Troops returned from the Western Front and the flying services no longer needed so many pilots. Smirnov was demobilised from the RAF, and to avoid being numbered among the numerous unemployed he became a member of a Russian officers' military organisation. Sent to Netheravon, on Salisbury Plain, he became a flying instructor, training Russian pilots to fly Bristol Fighters, Sopwith Snipes and Camels and DH 9s. After a few months the flying school was closed, and together with other Russian pilots Smirnov sailed for the south of Russia on a steamship put at Gen Anton Denikin's disposal – the latter was commander of the 'White Army' fighting the Bolshevik Red Army.

The ship arrived at Novorossiysk in late August 1919. Here, Smirnov met his old friend Lipsky, who told him of the catastrophic situation facing Denikin's Volunteer Army, and the imminent arrival of the Red Army in Novorossiysk. Lipsky advised Smirnov to get away from the doomed 'White Army' as quickly as possible. The next day Smirnov stowed away on the first departing steamship, and before the end of the civil war in Russia he had become the assistant to the attaché of the Military Air Fleet and chief pilot for the exiled Russian government in Paris.

Smirnov then spent some time in England, employed by the Handley Page company in its factory in Croydon. Apparently this work did not suit him, for he joined Belgian airline SNETA (ancestor of Sabena) a short while later as a pilot, flying passenger-carrying SPADs and DH 9s. However, a fire in one of the company's hangars destroyed Smirnov's machine, leaving him unemployed. Packing his modest luggage, he set off for Holland, where he managed to get work as a commercial pilot with KLM (Royal Dutch Airlines). Smirnov would remain with the company for more than 25 years.

On 19 October 1923 Smirnov took off from Schiphol Airport with three passengers in a Fokker F III. Strong winds and engine failure due to a faulty radiator necessitated a forced landing on the Goodwin Sands in the English Channel, and the coal steamer *Primo* rescued them just minutes before the

Fokker was submerged by the waves of the incoming tide. After that Ivan Smirnov was nicknamed 'Earl of the Goodwins'.

In 1928 Smirnov became the first KLM pilot to fly the postal route from Amsterdam to the Dutch East Indies and back – a distance of some 18,000 miles. During 1933-34 he flew this route in record time in Fokker F XVIII *Pelikaan* (Pelican). In 1940 Smirnov was permanently posted to the Dutch East Indies, where he continued to fly for KLM.

Following the Japanese attack on Pearl Harbor, Smirnov again donned military uniform and was enlisted as a captain in the army aviation corps of the Netherlands East Indies. There was heavy fighting in the east, and when Dutch forces retreated before the advancing Japanese army, Smirnov had to fly VIPs, women and children to Australia. They often escaped only minutes before the airfield was occupied by Japanese troops.

Smirnov did not return from the flight of 2 March 1942, his Douglas DC-3 PK-AKV being attacked in the region of Broome, on the Western Australian coast, by three Japanese Mitsubishi A6M Zero-sen fighters. Wounded by five bullets in his arm, Smirnov threw the aeroplane into an abrupt spiral, broke away from his attackers and made a forced landing on a sandy beach. They were found there five days later, all of the crew and passengers, bar four men, being rescued. The damaged aeroplane and its valuable cargo were recovered. However a small bag containing diamonds was never found.

Ivan Smirnov was later attached to the US Air Transport Command Headquarters in Brisbane, Queensland, and he flew as a captain in the 317th Troop Carrier Group. He continued to fly despite official attempts to ground him because of his age and his wounds. After World War 2 Smirnov returned to KLM as its senior pilot. When doctors finally forbade him from flying, Smirnov remained with the airline as its chief adviser. In his long flying career he spent more than 30,000 hrs in the air. Ivan Smirnov died in Palma de Mallorca on 28 October 1956. On 20 November 1959 he was reburied on Dutch soil in the cemetery at Heemstede.

Nikolai Kokorin

Nikolai Kokorin was born on 8 May 1889 in Khlebnikovo, a small town near Moscow. At the age of 21 he was conscripted, and first served as a soldier in the Vislenskaya River Mine Company. From October 1911 Kokorin continued his military service in aviation. At that time Russian military aviation was still in its infancy, not being a separate organisation within the army. Before the war Kokorin was promoted from motor mechanic to pilot-soldier. On 20 September 1914, when fighting was already in full swing, Kokorin, with the rank of Starshyi Unter-Officer (senior non-commissioned officer), passed his pilot's test on a Nieuport monoplane and was sent to the front.

In December he was transferred to the 4th KAO, where he proved to be an excellent scout pilot. For courageous reconnaissance flights and the successful bombing of enemy positions from March 1915 to June 1916, Kokorin was decorated with all four soldier's Crosses of St George. The future Russian ace also had his first air combats at that time, a 4th KAO report noting that 'on 14 April 1916 pilot Unter-Officer Kokorin and observer Podporuchik Belokurov, armed only with revolvers during deep rear reconnaissance on an MS type L, attacked an Albatros and drove it

Future five-victory ace Starshyi Unter-Officer Nikolai Kokorin of the 4th KAO was awarded the George Cross Fourth, Third and Second Class for successful reconnaissance flights in 1915-16

A Nieuport 11 built by the Dux factory in Moscow. The skull and crossbones emblem of the 1st BAG is clearly visible on its fin. Kokorin gained his first victory flying Nieuport 11 N1102, which was identical in appearance to this machine

Kokorin, second from the right, near the wreckage of a German Albatros C III that he shot down near Vul'ka Porskaya on 20 December 1916 whilst flying Morane-Saulnier Type I MS750

away. During the air combat Belokurov was wounded in the face'. The two men subsequently completed their reconnaissance tasking and returned to their airfield.

In recognition of his service to his country, Kokorin was promoted to Praporshchik by the Western Front Commander-in-Chief in Order No 275 of 25 August 1916, by which time his unit had joined the 1st BAG in the Lutsk region. As previously noted, this unit fought a series of fierce aerial battles with superior enemy forces in 1916-17, its pilots making tens of operational flights a day. The group soon achieved air superiority in the region, with Kokorin's contribution to this goal coming in the form of his first victory on 12 November 1916.

Having taken off in Nieuport 11 N1102, he soon saw a German two-seat reconnaissance aeroplane over the Russian rear and resolutely attacked it. The German observer returned fire with his machine gun, but Kokorin continued to close on the enemy machine and hit it numerous times. The attack lasted no more than 15 minutes, Kokorin wounding the German pilot and forcing him to land between Rozhishche and Kol Mikhalin in territory controlled by the Special Army in the Russian rear. For this deed Nikolai Kokorin was awarded the Gold Sword for Bravery (renamed the Order for the Army and the Navy from 31 July 1917).

Between 1100 hrs and 1300 hrs on 20 December 1916, volunteer pilot Smirnov and observer Shtabs-Kapitan Pentko in a Nieuport 10 and pilot Praporshchik Kokorin in Morane-Saulnier Type I MS750 brought down two enemy aeroplanes in the Lutsk region. These engagements took place over the frontline, and both enemy aircraft fell in locations occupied by Russian troops just 1.5 km (one mile) apart. The enemy airmen (three officers and one unteroffizier) were killed in the air by machine gun fire.

Kokorin had taken off at 1230 hrs in MS750 and then circled over Popovichi. Having noticed shell bursts from Russian artillery to the south of Linevka, he soon spotted an Albatros C III heading north. As Kokorin flew towards it, he saw the German cross on the right side of its fuselage. He attacked the enemy on a collision course at a height of 2200 m (7200 ft), his opponent being 50 m (160 ft) below him. After Kokorin's first burst of machine gun fire the German pilot turned to the left, thus making himself vulnerable to attack from the right. After the second burst Kokorin attacked the enemy machine from above and behind, at which point the Albatros began to glide down sharply, trailing a jet of steam from its punctured radiator.

After descending no more than 150 m (500 ft), the aircraft side-slipped on its right wing and turned over, whereupon the pilot and observer fell out. The aircraft fell in the region of Vul'ka-Porskaya, 500 m (550 yards) from the staff of the 222nd Regiment, and Kokorin landed nearby. Examination of the corpses revealed that the pilot had been wounded in the stomach and both thighs. The officer-observer was killed by a bullet that passed right through his breast.

For this combat Kokorin was awarded the Order of St George 4th Class (also renamed the Order for the Army and the Navy from 31 July 1917). He was subsequently decorated with the Order of St Anne 4th Class for Bravery (Southwest Front Order No 111, dated 26 January 1917) and the Order of St Stanislaw 3rd Class with Crossed Swords and Bow (Southwest Front Order No 454 of 13 April 1917). By then Kokorin was an experienced pilot, having mastered several types of aircraft. He was also regarded as an authority by his comrades-in-arms. In the spring of 1917 the 1st BAG commander, military pilot Shtabs-Rotmistr Alexander Kozakov, recommended him as an 'excellent and fearless fighter pilot, capable of flying all aircraft types. A brave officer, he is well qualified in his field'.

Kokorin soon justified his commander's trust, shooting down a German aeroplane near Kozovo on 1 April 1917. Again at the controls of MS750, he had taken off at 0545 hrs to patrol the region of Vychulki-Halich-Brzeżany-Kozovo-Uvse – it was his second sortie that day. At 3500 m (11,500 ft) near Kozovo, Kokorin saw two Albatros C IIIs. The first continued to fly in a northeasterly direction, while the second

Nikolai Kokorin shot down five enemy two-seat reconnaissance aircraft between 12 November 1916 and 12 May 1917

Kokorin is seen here standing with his hands in his pockets alongside a German Albatros C III that he had shot down near Kozova on 1 April 1917. The future ace shared this success with squadronmate Mladshyi Unter-Offizer Mikhail Zemblevich, even though the latter had attacked the enemy machine only once, opening fire from too far away and withdrawing soon after

turned to the west, heading towards the frontline. The leading aeroplane then turned towards Kokorin, who was above his opponent. The Russian descended steeply to meet the Albatros C III head on, at which point the enemy pilot made a 90-degree turn and began to descend. His observer fired at the Morane, but this did not prevent Kokorin from attacking his opponent several times and forcing the aircraft to land three kilometres (two miles) to the west of Uvse village.

During the forced landing the enemy aeroplane nosed over. Kokorin alighted nearby, and upon inspecting his victim he found that the aircraft and its petrol tank had been holed many times by the rounds he had fired, and that the enemy pilot had been hit by three bullets. He and his unharmed officer-observer were taken prisoner. The Albatros C III, fitted with a 168 hp Mercedes engine, was damaged when it nosed over. This success gave Kokorin his third victory.

Another pilot from the same squadron, Mladshyi Unter-Officer Mikhail Zemblevich, flying Nieuport 21 N2195, also took part in this action, but he had attacked the enemy only once, opening fire from too far away and withdrawing soon after.

For his successful combats and long period of service at the front, Kokorin was given a well-deserved rest, and he went on leave on 7 April. Just 24 hours after returning to his unit, he claimed his fourth victory. Six fighters of the 4th KAO took off on late morning patrol on 11 May, and at 1210 hrs Kokorin (flying Nieuport 21 N1810) engaged an enemy machine. Patrolling at 3700 m (12,000 ft), he saw and attacked the German aeroplane over the frontline at 3300 m (10,800 ft) near Shibalin village. During the combat the enemy machine descended from 3300 m to 1000 m (3300 ft). After Kokorin's attacks the enemy aircraft dived and fell probably between Shibalin and Brzeżany. The Russian pilot lost sight of his quarry and returned home.

The 41st AK report from the frontline states 'an enemy aeroplane was overtaken, machine gunned by our fighter and forced to descend in Brzeżany Forest at Kotuv, in enemy-held territory'. According to Austrian archives, Hansa-Brandenburg C I 64.62 of *Flik* 11 was attacked by a single Russian fighter that day. The pilot, Knotis, and observer Franz Fasching were seriously wounded and made a forced landing behind their own trenches.

The following day Kokorin gained his fifth victory, again flying N1810. He was on patrol with Praporshchik Zemblevich when they attacked and shot down Hansa-Brandenburg C I 64.51 of *Flik* 9 over Kozovo. The reconnaissance machine fell near the village of Teofipulka and was destroyed. Its observer, Oberleutnant Richard Rack, fell from his cockpit at 1500 m (4900 ft) and the pilot, Michael Berger, was killed during the combat.

On 16 May pilots of the 1st BAG performed 13 operational flights and were involved in five combats. On that day Praporshchik Kokorin of the 4th KAO died a hero's death in an encounter with three enemy aeroplanes that commenced over Podhaice at 0520 hrs. He was killed by an armour-piercing bullet that penetrated his body near his right shoulder blade bone and passed through his left shoulder. Nieuport 21 N1810 fell three kilometres (two miles) from Podhaice at 0600 hrs and was destroyed. German pilot Ltn Grybski of *Flieger Abteilung* 242 was probably the victor, as according to German archive records he claimed to have shot down a Russian single-seat Nieuport that day, which fell to the east of Podhaice.

Thus ended the career of Russian ace Nikolai Kokorin. Just over two months later, on 22 July 1917, military pilot Kokorin of the 4th KAO was promoted to the rank of podporuchik. This order had reached the squadron too late to be enacted.

ACES OF THE 7th AOI

Vasily Yanchenko

Born on 1 January 1894 in the village of Nikolsk-Ussuriisk in far east Russia, Vasily Yanchenko graduated from Saratov secondary technical school and at the beginning of World War 1 joined the Guards Aviation Detachment on the Southwest Front as a volunteer. Having completed aviation courses at the Petrograd Polytechnic Institute on 3 April 1915, he was assigned to the Sevastopol Flying School. On 24 August that same year he graduated from the flying school as a pilot and was transferred to the 12th KAO. Following a number of successful combat missions with this unit the young pilot was awarded the soldier's St George Cross 4th and 3rd Class and given the rank of Starshyi Unter-Officer.

On 23 December 1915 Yanchenko was transferred to the 3rd KAO, and three months later he requested a posting to fighter aviation. Assigned to the 7th AOI, he served with such success in this unit during July and August 1916 that he was awarded the soldier's St George Cross 2nd and 1st Class and promoted to Praporshchik.

That summer the pilots of the 7th AOI had been engaged in aerial combat over the Brzeżany-Halych-Bolshovtsy-Buchach sector of the front. On 8 July, in accordance with a 2nd AK order, Yanchenko was awarded the soldier's St George Cross 2nd Class No 10528 'for air combat with enemy aeroplanes'. In August he was awarded soldier's St George Cross 1st Class No 11362 for an action on 12 June. On that day, flying Nieuport 10 N292, he intercepted an enemy reconnaissance aircraft and repeatedly attacked it. With machine gun fire he drove the aircraft away from its position and forced it to descend towards Podhaice in a steep banking turn.

For his outstanding service Yanchenko gained his first officer's award in September 1916 – the Order of St Anne 4th Class, with the legend 'For Bravery', and the status of military pilot. On 22 September, 7th AOI pilots Yanchenko and Orlov shot down an enemy aircraft over Brzeżany. Firing tracer bullets, they set the aircraft alight and it descended in the Złota Lipa region enveloped in black smoke – it fell behind the enemy trenches. No confirmation of this victory has been found in Austrian or German archives, however.

At 1605 hrs during his second patrol on 2 October (or 4 October according to other sources), Praporshchik Yanchenko – again in Nieuport 11 N1302 – saw three enemy aeroplanes over Lipitsa-Gurna, in the Svistel'niki-Potutory region. After his initial attack, one of his opponents fled back over enemy territory, but the other two joined battle. Yanchenko managed to hit one of the aircraft, which began to glide towards the frontline, while the other machine broke off for home. For this combat

When this photograph of Praporshchik Vasily Yanchenko of the 7th AOI was taken in September 1916 he had yet to claim any of his nine victories

Nieuports of the 7th AOI at Vikturovka airfield in early June 1917. Nieuport 11 N1232, in the centre, is fitted with a Lewis machine gun on its upper wing. On 31 March 1917 Yanchenko had used this aircraft to down a Hansa-Brandenburg C I for his third confirmed victory. N1232, which the ace had flown from August 1916 through to April 1917, was subsequently written-off in a crash on 27 July 1917 while being flown by Podporuchik Sakovich

Yanchenko was awarded the Order of St Vladimir 4th Class with Crossed Swords and Bow, as notified in Southwestern Front Order No 2028 of 21 December 1916, and he was also given ten days' leave.

On 22 February 1917, 7th AOI pilots Poruchik Donat Makijonek and Praporshchik Vasily Yanchenko (flying Nieuport 21 N1889) shot down a two-seat Albatros reconnaissance aircraft over Svistel'niki village. The Russian pilots carried out eight attacks in the 20-minute engagement, the stricken machine falling in enemy lines to the west of Lipitsa-Gurna.

Pilots of the 7th AOI engaged several enemy reconnaissance aircraft on 31 March, bringing down two of them. The first of these was shot down by Yanchenko and Donat Makijonek near Lysiec. After their joint attacks over Bohorodczany, the enemy machine caught fire and crashed into a forest to the west of Majdanska Buda. It was later discovered that their victim was Hansa-Brandenburg C I 67.03 of *Flik* 7, crewed by pilot Fw Paul Hablitschek and observer Oblt Roman Schmidt.

Yanchenko then attacked another aeroplane over Posech village together with Kornet Gilsher. The former attacked from out of the sun, which made him barely visible to the enemy. Approaching to within 20 m (60 yd), he opened fire. After this devastating attack, the enemy aircraft descended in a steep spiral, with Yanchenko pursuing him, firing short bursts. The enemy observer soon stopped firing back, and the machine tipped onto a wing, descended steeply and disappeared behind a forest west of Puste Pole. Confirmation soon came from Podporuchik Chernyaev of the 12th AK staff;

'At 1525 hrs a hostile aeroplane streaming black smoke fell into the forest in the direction of Posech village.'

According to Austrian archives, on that day an aeroplane from *Flik* 7 fell after an encounter with a Russian fighter. Observer Ltn Szeliga was wounded in both legs, but Feldpilot Zgf Klefac was unhurt, landing his damaged aircraft with difficulty. This was almost certainly the machine shot down by Yanchenko and Gilsher.

Exactly two weeks later Yanchenko was patrolling over the frontline in Morane-Saulnier Type I MS745 when the aircraft was hit by enemy anti-aircraft fire, damaging the fighter and slightly wounding the pilot in the legs. Yanchenko forced-landed a short while later behind Russian trenches.

On 14 June Yanchenko took off in Nieuport 21 N1889 from Vikturovka airfield to patrol in the region of Kozova-Shibalin-Podhaice-Shumlyany. Seeing three enemy aircraft heading towards Podhaice, he set off in pursuit. Catching up with one of them over Shumlyany, he opened fire. After several passes his opponent rapidly lost altitude, but Yanchenko failed to locate any wreckage.

Five days later, flying the same fighter, he twice attacked enemy aeroplanes. Again, one of his opponents fell out of formation and headed for Brzeżany, on the enemy side of the lines. Yanchenko later reported, 'I attacked and shot down an enemy spotter aeroplane. During its fall it turned over in the air several times'. He claimed that the enemy aircraft fell west of Adamuvka in the region of Potutory. Like Yanchenko's opponent on 14 June, this victory remained unconfirmed.

On 23 June, again at the controls of N1889, Yanchenko was ordered to photograph hostile artillery batteries northeast of Brzeżany. Poruchik Makijonek, in Nieuport 17 N2453, escorted him. When Yanchenko commenced his photo runs, a two-seat enemy aeroplane attempted to attack him. The aircraft was quickly despatched, however, by Yanchenko and Makijonek, the stricken machine falling in enemy territory to the north of Brzeżany.

Five days later the same two pilots were patrolling over the Kozovo-Kuropatniki-Brzeżany sector when they saw, and attacked, four enemy aeroplanes. One of these machines was seen to descend enveloped in thick smoke. Given a shared credit for the aeroplane's demise, Yanchenko was now an ace.

On 5 July, again flying N1889, he chased an enemy aeroplane until he caught up with it over Brzeżany. Making a firing pass at the machine, Yanchenko saw it drop away steeply trailing a thick plume of smoke until it disappeared into a forest close to the highway to the northwest of Brzeżany.

Two days later pilots Kornet Gilsher, Poruchik Makijonek and Praporshchik Yanchenko of the 7th AOI took off to repel an attack on Tarnopol by eight enemy aeroplanes. Makijonek became involved in a fight with one of the hostile machines as it moved away from the target area, while Yanchenko and Gilsher attacked and shot down an enemy aeroplane. Several other machines then attacked Gilsher's aeroplane and he was shot down. Yanchenko went into a spin in order to avoid the same fate, this manoeuvre allowing him to break off the fight. Minutes later he landed alongside the wreckage of Gilsher's aircraft. Having removed the body of his squadronmate from the shattered fighter, the ace ordered soldiers to take it to the 7th AOI's airfield.

On 24 August Yanchenko made two sorties, and during the second one he saw an Austrian Hansa-Brandenburg armed with two machine guns over Satunovo. The enemy pilot attacked first, and he was evidently skilled at aerobatics. Every time Yanchenko attacked, his opponent made a steep turn, preventing the Russian pilot from getting him in his sights. After a 20-minute engagement the enemy pilot descended behind his own trenches and escaped.

In September Yanchenko was transferred to the 32nd KAO, where he was assigned Nieuport 23 N3374. On the 8th of that month he took off to escort aircraft sent to photograph enemy positions. At an altitude of

5200 m (17,000 ft) to the west of Husiatyn he intercepted an enemy Albatros. After his second attack the machine descended steeply and crashed in the Chebaruvka region. During the engagement Yanchenko had pursued the enemy aeroplane down to 2000 m (6500 ft).

Two days later he took off to escort a reconnaissance aeroplane in the same region, and over Husiatyn he saw an enemy Albatros fighter trying to down a Russian Farman. Yanchenko attacked the aeroplane at 1120 hrs, the ace later reporting that his opponent was flying a single-seat Albatros fighter of yellowish colour, with the crosses on its rudder and fuselage outlined in white. Black crosses on a circular white background were painted on the wings. After a ten-minute combat in which the enemy pilot demonstrated his agility, the Albatros descended steeply in the region of Chebaruvka and flew away.

On 26 September Yanchenko took off to escort a scout that was reconnoitring Zhishchinzy-Husiatyn-Zbrizh. Over Zbrizh at 3000 m (9800 ft), he saw an enemy Aviatik two-seater attacking a Russian reconnaissance aircraft. Yanchenko quickly despatched the enemy machine, expending 380 bullets to shoot it down. The Aviatik crashed onto the right bank of the Zbruch River, close to the small town of Zbrizh, in enemy territory. The crash site was confirmed in a reconnaissance report by the Southwestern Front staff dated 27 September 1917.

Yanchenko's ninth, and last, victory came on the 7th Army front on 1 October when Albatros D III 53.20, fitted with a 165 hp engine, was shot down east of Kutkovtsy. He described the victory as follows;

'Having escorted Farman biplanes to Olkhovets village, I continued to patrol in the Zbizh-Husiatyn region. At 1630 hrs I noticed four enemy aeroplanes heading to our rear at Horodok. I engaged them in combat, first attacking a single-seat Albatros, which was somewhat higher than the group. In a steep turn, I fired at the enemy from point-blank range, and could see my bullets piercing his wings. I was then attacked by the other enemy aeroplanes, which forced me to turn on a wing and fall into a spin.

'After dropping some 200-300 m [650-980 ft], I levelled my aeroplane off and saw other enemy machines over Horodok, heading for Kutkovtsy. I started to pursue them, and over Dubrovka Farm caught up with a single-seat Albatros flying ahead of me off to my right. I attacked it from above and to the left, as the enemy was performing a steep turn in that direction in an effort to meet me head-on. After I had fired my machine gun the enemy aircraft side-slipped, descended steeply and crashed at the edge of a wood near Dubrovka Farm. I landed nearby and found broken pieces of the aeroplane and the dead officer-pilot. I handed his documents over to the 7th Siberian Army Corps staff.'

According to the *Casualty List of German Air Forces During the First World War* (*Verlustliste Deutschen Luftstreitkräfte in Weltkrieg*, Berlin, 1930), on 1 October 1917 Ltn d R Martin Schön was killed in action. The location of his death, Zyszczyncy (Russland) or Zhishchinzy, coincides with the patrol area of Yanchenko at that time. It is therefore very likely that it was Schön's Albatros that Yanchenko shot down. Shtabs-Rotmistr Grochowalski also claimed that he shot down an aircraft at this time, but that he lost sight of it after his second attack and did not see it crash.

On 16 October Yanchenko was patrolling in the Zhishchinzy-Husiatyn-Zbizh region when he saw an enemy two-seater at 4000 m (13,000 ft) over Ivankovtsy. Making a frontal attack, he fired 500 bullets and the enemy aeroplane descended steeply down to 600 m (1950 ft) with its engine running and then flew away to the rear, manoeuvring as it went. Yanchenko noted that the two-seater was of a new type, with greatly tapered wingtips (perhaps it was an Ago C IV). The aircraft was camouflaged and flew at high speed. Yanchenko could not chase it down in his Nieuport 23, even with the throttle wide open and the fighter in a dive.

He made his last flight on the front on 29 October, finishing the war with the rank of Poruchik.

After the October Revolution Yanchenko became an active participant in the White Russian movement. During the Russian Civil War of 1918-20 he served with aviation units of the Volunteer Army of Gen Denikin and the Russian Army of Baron Wrangel. During 18 months of fighting in the hardest conditions imaginable, Yanchenko was described on several occasions in the command orders as being a brave and valiant pilot and a capable commander of the detachment. At the end of the Civil War he was promoted to the rank of Kapitan for successful combat operations. In June 1920 Yanchenko was nominated for the Order of St Nicholas Thaumaturge for battle honours. In the autumn of that same year Vasily Yanchenko was evacuated from the Crimea with Baron Wrangel's troops and left Russia forever.

Some years later Yanchenko arrived in the USA. For a short time he worked as an engineer with Igor Sikorsky's company, and in the late 1920s he became an American citizen. In the 1930s he moved to Syracuse, New York, where he worked as a design engineer until his retirement in 1952. Vasily Yanchenko passed away in Dade County, Florida, in August 1959, aged 65.

Donat Makijonek

Donat Makijonek was born on 19 May 1890. His parents were Polish peasants in the Dambovka village of Osvedskoy volost in the province of Vitebsk. In 1906 he graduated from a vocational technical school in Vitebsk, and at the age of 21 he was conscripted into the Russian Army. On 7 November 1911 Makijonek took the oath of the Russian Emperor Nikolai II and became a soldier of the 97th Infantry Liflandsky Regiment.

His career in aviation began on 21 March 1912, when he was transferred to the 3rd KAO of the 4th Aviation Company. Initially, Makijonek was a mechanic, but he then requested a transfer to flying school despite such training usually being reserved for officers only. On 28 May 1912 Makijonek was sent to Sevastopol Military Flying School, where he initially completed courses in motor mechanics and then worked for a time in this capacity at the school. He then joined a group of students that were being trained to fly the Nieuport IV monoplane. On 22 February 1914 Makijonek successfully graduated from Sevastopol Flying School with brevet No 239 and the title of pilot.

In March pilot-soldier Makijonek returned to the 3rd KAO, where he was steadily promoted – on 4 May he was given the rank of Efreitor

(Corporal), 15 days later he was made a Mladshy Unter-Officer and on 14 June he was promoted to Starshyi Unter-Officer. On 31 July, just 72 hours after the start of World War 1, Makijonek was posted to the eastern front with his detachment.

With the onset of war the 3rd KAO was attached to the staff of the 3rd AK of the 1st Army, which was fighting in Eastern Prussia. Commanded by Shtabs-Kapitan Georgy Myachkov, the 3rd KAO had five Nieuport IVs and eight officers (five pilots and three observers). The only pilot to have risen through the ranks was Makijonek.

On 8 August Makijonek, flying in difficult conditions, succeeded in finding units of the Guards cavalry corps of Gen Khan-Nakhichevansky and handing over an order to him from the 3rd AK commander. For accomplishing this task Makijonek received his first military award, the soldier's Cross of St George 4th Class.

In the second half of August Russian troops were stopped in their advance westward and then forced to retreat. In this situation the 3rd KAO pilots continued to support soldiers on the ground by performing reconnaissance flights over Königsberg, Allenburg and Frinland. As a consequence of this intensive work, the detachment's aircraft were in poor shape by the end of August, mainly owing to damage sustained during takeoffs and landings. Pilots from the 3rd KAO were duly sent to Moscow to collect new aircraft, and it was not until 10 December 1914 that the unit, now equipped with Morane-Saulnier Type Gs and Ls, returned to combat operations at the front.

In January 1915 the 3rd KAO continued its work over the 3rd AK front. Anti-aircraft fire presented a serious danger for pilots, and on 14 April, while Makijonek was making a reconnaissance flight over Kruglevitse in Type G MS107, a stray bullet hit his engine, which stopped. Makijonek turned towards Nida and began to glide in the direction of the Russian lines. He tried several times to start the engine, but without success. Under heavy fire, the aeroplane glided over the enemy trenches at a height of only 100-150 m (300-500 ft) and landed in the wetlands southwest of Simnikhov. The Morane turned over when it made contact with the ground, trapping observer Podporuchik Makeichik in his cockpit. Makijonek pulled him free and they crawled to the nearest trenches, which they reached just as heavy artillery opened fire and their aircraft was destroyed.

For his performance during this heroic flight and for rescuing Makeichik, Makijonek was awarded the soldier's Cross of St George 3rd Class No 21450 on 15 April 1915. The 25th AK commander visited the 3rd KAO and personally decorated the hero.

On 16 June 1915 Makijonek, with observer Poruchik Shirkov, spotted the movement of a considerable concentration of enemy troops in the Sandomir region, as well as the construction of a bridge across the San River. The Russian pilots quickly reported to the command that the enemy was preparing to attack, and for this Makijonek was awarded the Cross of St George 2nd Class (No 602). That month he was promoted in rank to Podpraporshchik (NCO) in recognition of his combat service. Makijonek's successful actions during the summer of 1915 eventually culminated in him being given his first officer rank on 21 September, when he became a Praporshchik for his valour.

In October the 3rd KAO moved to Odessa for a rest. For almost a month the pilots had a break from combat, making only training flights. On 29 November the 3rd KAO left Odessa by train for the 7th Army front, where it came under the command of the 1st AK staff. In the second half of December the detachment resumed combat operations from Verzhbovets airfield, and by an Imperial Order of 31 December Makijonek was conferred with the title of military pilot for war service.

On 15 March 1916 Makijonek took off alone to pursue an enemy aeroplane that had appeared over the village of Kosovo. Flying Morane-Saulnier Type L MS239, he caught up with the enemy machine over Haivoronka and pursued it to Podhaice. Near Leszowka village he forced the aircraft to descend in its own territory. This victory was not confirmed, however.

In accordance with Southwestern Front Order No 618 of 15 April 1916, Makijonek was awarded his first officer's order, the Order of St Vladimir 4th Class with Crossed Swords and Bow. That same year it was followed by other awards – the Order of St Stanislav 3rd Class with Crossed Swords and Bow, the Order of St Anne 3rd Class with Crossed Swords and Bow, the Order of St Anne 4th Class with inscription 'For Bravery' and the Order of St Stanislav 2nd Class with Crossed Swords.

By an Imperial Order of 30 July 1916, Makijonek was given the rank of Podporuchik. Deciding to devote himself to fighter aviation, he asked to be transferred from the 3rd KAO to the 7th AOI. Both detachments were part of the 7th AD, and his transfer took place by Order No 411 of 15 December 1916. Makijonek did not arrive at the 7th AOI until 19 January 1917, as he spent a short while in hospital receiving treatment. By an Imperial Order of 23 January 1917 he was promoted to a Poruchik of the engineer troops. After several training flights over the airfield Makijonek started making combat flights in February.

On 22 February he and Praporshchik Yanchenko of the 7th AOI intercepted an Albatros over Svistelniki village at 2200 m (7200 ft), and after a 20-minute fight shot it down in a joint attack. The aircraft fell in

Personnel of the 3rd KAO in the spring of 1916. They are, from left to right, V S Shustarev, Ya K Filonov, F G Fedorov, D Makijonek, A Fedotov, N N Rybaltovsky, A G Belyaev, A V Shiukov and A A Gudkov. Of these men, only Donat Makijonek would 'make ace', claiming nine victories and being officially credited with five of them

59

A rare in-flight photograph of a Nieuport 11 from the 7th AOI on a patrol over the Southwest Front in the spring of 1917

a field in enemy-held territory to the west of Lipica Górna village. During the combat Yanchenko had descended to 400 m (1300 ft) and Makijonek to 800 m (2600 ft). For the latter (flying Nieuport 11 N1679), it was the first victory that could be confirmed. Although the aeroplane fell in enemy territory, the victory was mentioned in detachment and division orders.

Makijonek gained his next victory on 31 March 1917, again in N1679. After taking off at 0845 hrs to pursue an enemy aeroplane in the Tyśmienica-Stanisławów region, he saw two aircraft over Bohorodczany. Drawing near, he discovered that one was a Russian Morane, pursued by an enemy Hansa-Brandenburg C I. Makijonek attacked the hostile machine over Lysiec, causing the enemy pilot to stop pursuing the Morane and engage him instead. During the fight another Morane appeared on the scene, piloted by Yanchenko, who attacked the enemy aircraft and forced it to descend. It was then Makijonek's turn to fire at the C I, which rolled over onto a wing and crashed into a forest to the west of the Majdanska Buda, bursting into flames when it hit the ground. A telegram from the 117th Infantry Division staff confirmed the demise of the enemy aircraft following combat with Russian pilots, and this information was printed in the official report of the Supreme Command staff.

According to Austrian archives their victim was C I 67.03 of *Flik* 7, which was shot down in the Bohorodczany area by a Russian Nieuport on 13 April. Its pilot, Fw Paul Hablitschek, was wounded in the hip. The observer, Oblt Roman Schmidt, tried to make a forced landing at the 14th Aeronautic Company's airfield, but the aircraft was destroyed in the crash. Hablitschek later died of his wounds on 26 May.

In the Jamnica region on 14 April Makijonek intercepted an enemy aircraft. After his first attack it banked over on a wing and landed near Kozyarki village. This claim is mentioned only in Makijonek's mission report, and was not officially confirmed as a victory because his opponent descended in enemy territory.

In May the intensity of combat action by 7th AOI pilots remained high. Of 105 sorties made by five pilots of the detachment that month, no fewer than 30 were undertaken by Makijonek. Indeed, on some days he flew two or three missions in Nieuport 21 N1990.

June saw an offensive launched on the 7th Army front, this proving to be the last attempt by the Provisional government to retake territory lost to the enemy. However, strict discipline was already absent in the trenches, with soldiers' committees giving the orders in combatant units. Whole regiments left the trenches and moved to the rear, refusing to fight. Under these conditions the Russian offensive was doomed to failure. Only the artillery and aviation units were combat-ready, and they maintained a high operational tempo under the severest of conditions.

In June the pilots of the 7th AOI made 146 combat flights, 39 of which were flown by Makijonek in either N1990 or Nieuport 17 N2453 (both machines being French-built). He gained his next victory, in N1990, on

16 June when he attacked a two-seater in the Shibalin-Potutory region and it descended steeply and forced-landed behind the enemy trenches near Marzenyuvka Farm. While he was distracted by the demise of his opponent, Makijonek was suddenly attacked by two more enemy aeroplanes and his Nieuport badly damaged. With difficulty, he landed behind the Russian trenches, where he found that the wings of his fighter had been pierced in six places and the rudder control damaged. In addition, the lower wing was broken during the forced landing. Makijonek's victory was later confirmed by ground forces and mentioned in official reports.

On 23 June Poruchik Makijonek took off in N2453 to escort Praporshchik Yanchenko in Nieuport 21 N1889, who was tasked with photographing enemy batteries northeast of Brzeżany. While he was taking his photographs Yanchenko was engaged by an enemy aeroplane, which was shot down by the combined attacks of Yanchenko and Makijonek. The two-seater fell in enemy territory near Lapszyn village, to the north of Brzeżany, the Russians' victory being confirmed by the ground troops. These successes resulted in Makijonek being nominated for the Order of St George 4th Class, which he received in the autumn of 1917.

Makijonek and Yanchenko again attacked enemy aircraft on 28 June when four hostile machines were spotted at 2400 m (7900 ft) over Brzeżany. After several attacks the enemy aeroplanes began to retreat, one of them descending enveloped in dense smoke. Although this incident was recorded in the detachment and division documentation, and both Makijonek and Yanchenko were awarded victories, the final fate of the aircraft remained inconclusive because it fell in enemy territory.

Eleven days earlier, on 17 June, the 7th AOI's commander, Podporuchik Ivan Orlov, had died a hero's death. For Donat Makijonek he had been both a commander and a comrade-in-arms. In a testimonial written just prior to his death, Orlov had written of Makijonek;

'A pilot of astonishing courage. He not only carries out orders perfectly, but he always volunteers for dangerous missions, which he performs brilliantly. He has a calm and communicative nature, most suitable for fighter work, although he will perform any tasks equally well.'

Kornet Yuri Gilsher was appointed the new commander of the 7th AOI, but he too was killed in action on 7 July. In the wake of his death Poruchik Makijonek began to perform the duties of the detachment commander. He led the unit for about a month, setting a worthy example for his

Makijonek, second from left, poses with his Nieuport 17 at Vikturovka airfield on the Southwest Front in June 1917. The 7th AOI had taken delivery of this aeroplane (N2453) from the 7th AD just days prior this photograph being taken, and it was flown in combat up to November of that year. Note the personal insignia painted on the fighter's fuselage and tail, as well as the nose cone fitted to the propeller hub. Makijonek was N2453's first assigned pilot, and he flew it until September, when the fighter was passed on to Podporuchik Nyukyanen. Its total combat flying time was 94 hours and 15 minutes

Kapitan Donat Makijonek as a pilot of the 1st Polish aviation detachment in 1919. Having served as a soldier from 1911 through to 1920, surviving six years of combat during that time, Makijonek subsequently perished in the concentration camp at Auschwitz during World War 2, the exact date of his death being unknown

comrades to follow. On 6 August Makijonek made his last flight. He took off (in N2453) from Husyatin airfield on a patrol, and over Olchowce at 3500 m (11,500 ft) he attacked an enemy aeroplane and pursued it in a dive down to 400 m (1300 ft), when his machine gun jammed. The damaged enemy aircraft flew across the frontline and made an emergency landing near Chabarowka. Having freed his machine gun, Makijonek then attacked another aircraft and forced it down on the enemy airfield near the village of Kopyczynce. As both machines landed in enemy-held territory, official confirmation of these victories has not been found.

On 11 August Makijonek fell ill, and was replaced as commander of the 7th AOI by military pilot Shtabs-Rotmistr Grochowalski. On 6 September Makijonek was assigned to the pilot-observers school at Evpatoria, in the Crimea, to 'study machine gun techniques'. This was in fact a formal pretext to send him to the rear for treatment. He never reached the Evpatoria school, as on 17 September, immediately upon his arrival in south Russia, he was admitted to the Sevastopol Red Cross Hospital. Makijonek remained there for a month, by which time he had been promoted to the rank of Shtabs-Kapitan by an Army and Navy Order dated 27 September 1917.

In November, having finally completed the short-term machine gun courses in Evpatoria, Makijonek was sent to Petrograd and placed at the disposal of the head of the Aviation and Aeronautics Department. By this time the Bolsheviks had seized power, and the Department's work was paralysed, so at the end of November, with the rank of Kapitan, Makijonek returned to the 7th AOI. Shortly thereafter he submitted an application for transfer to the Polish Corps, on the basis of the Supreme Committee order for the uniting of military Poles with the 7th Army.

On 5 January 1918 Kapitan Donat Makijonek of the Russian Army, together with his mechanic, flew to Kamieniec-Podolsk. The 1st Polish aviation detachment was formed there a short while later, and Makijonek was appointed assistant to the unit commander. During the Russian Civil War of 1918-20 he participated in combat on other fronts as a Polish Army pilot.

Donat Makijonek made nearly 600 combat flights during his flying career, participated in more than 30 aerial engagements and shot down nine enemy aeroplanes, five of which were officially confirmed. He mastered 14 types of aircraft. After starting service as a soldier in the autumn of 1911, in six years of service in both war and peace Makijonek had risen to the rank of Kapitan. For the heroism he displayed over the World War 1 battlefields, he was presented with many Russian awards, namely the soldier of St George Cross of all four classes and seven officer's orders, including the highest, the Order of St George 4th Class. Allied Serbia awarded him the Order of the Orla Bialego 4th Class, and Poland subsequently decorated him with the Virtuti Militari 5th Class, Krzyz Walecznych, Medaille de la Victoire and the Krzyz Niepodleglosci.

Polish historian Tomasz Kopanski told the author that Makijonek subsequently died in the concentration camp at Auschwitz during World War 2, the exact date of his death being unknown. An ace of the Russian Imperial Military Air Fleet, Donat Makijonek had survived World War 1 and the Russian Civil War only to disappear without trace in a giant furnace of World War 2 that consumed millions of people.

Ivan Orlov

Born in Petrograd province on 6 January 1895 into a family of gentry, Ivan Orlov received his secondary education in the Imperial Alexandrovsky Lyceum, where the young student displayed a great interest in aviation. A budding aeronautical engineer, his early design work resulted in the construction of the Orlov No 1 monoplane, powered by a 35 hp Anzani engine. He learned to fly in this machine, with flight testing of the aircraft and flying training being conducted simultaneously! Shortly before the war Orlov graduated from the flying school of the Imperial All-Russian Aero Club, where, on 31 May 1914, he was awarded pilot-aviator brevet No 229.

Before enlistment Orlov was a student at Petrograd University, but with the beginning of the war he volunteered immediately after the announcement of mobilisation. On 20 July 1914 Orlov handed in his application, and the following day he was enlisted in the 5th KAO. On 27 July, after a parting prayer, a detachment of six officers and 138 soldiers left for the front from Warsaw station in Petrograd. Orlov's unit was equipped with six Farman F 22bis biplanes, fitted with 80 hp Gnome engines. Interestingly, pilot-volunteer Ivan Orlov joined the 5th KAO in his own Farman S 7.

The unit was under the command of the 20th AK of the Northwest Front 1st Army, and it took part in the infamous East Prussian operation. Frontline aviation had 56 aeroplanes and two dirigibles available for the offensive, which Gen Samsonov's 1st Army launched on 4 August. However, German forces succeeded in stopping the Russian troops, and then commenced a counteroffensive of their own. The advancing German troops forced the Russian armies of the Northwestern Front to withdraw to their initial positions. Nearly 30,000 Russians were encircled, and on the night of 17 August Gen Samsonov committed suicide to avoid captivity.

Orlov made his first military flight on 7 August, reconnoitring the area around the city of Stalupenen. In all, he made 18 combat flights in August, earning him his first military award for successful reconnaissance missions in the region of Königsberg. In accordance with 20th AK Order No 26 of 20 August 1914, Orlov was awarded soldier's St George Cross 4th Class No 5661.

After his enlistment in the squadron, Orlov enjoyed steady promotion through the ranks. On 1 September he was given the rank of Efreitor, and 20 days later he was made a Mladshy Unter-Officer. In 1st Army Order of the day No 263 of 18 November 1914 Orlov was awarded soldier's St George Cross 3rd Class No 11312 'for aerial reconnaissance on 4 October in the region of Vyshtenets lake-Verzhblovo and the destruction of a railway by bombing'.

By the end of 1914 Orlov was serving on the staff of the 5th KAO. For organising communication with the 2nd Army headquarters staff on 8 November, pilot-volunteer Ivan Orlov was awarded soldier's St George Cross 2nd Class No 4720. On 12 December he left the detachment for a well-deserved period of leave, after which he was sent to Petrograd Flying School for training.

In accordance with Northwest Front Order of the day No 474 of 22 January 1915, Orlov was awarded the rank of Praporshchik for military

Five-victory ace Ivan Orlov was decorated with three soldier's Crosses of St George, attained the rank of Praporshchik and was nominated for the Order of St Anna 4th Class with the inscription 'For bravery'

merits. In February he was assigned to the 1st Army Aviation Detachment (AO), and he arrived there from Warsaw in Voisin biplane s/n 99 on 31 March. The 1st Army AO was attached to the 12th Army staff and located on an airfield not far from Snyadovo. Orlov's usual combat work started again – reconnaissance and bombing missions – and he also participated in his first aerial engagements.

One such clash took place on 13 May, when several Russian pilots took off on patrol – Praporshchik Orlov and observer Poruchik Okulich-Kazarinov in a Voisin armed with a machine gun, 14th KAO pilot Poruchik Korovnikov and observer Poruchik Danich in a Nieuport 10 armed with a Mauser pistol and 4th Siberian KAO Starshyi Unter-Officer Voronin in a Nieuport, also armed with a Mauser. At 0800 hrs, at an altitude of 2000 m (6500 ft), the Russian pilots saw a German Albatros over Chervony Bor, flying towards Snyadovo, and attacked it. The enemy aircraft was shot down, descending behind the lines near Novgorod.

According to archive records, Oblt Reinhold Rosenbaum and Ltn Walter Wittke of *Flieger Abteilung* 15 were wounded that day during a sortie in the region of Snyadovo-Kolno. Rosenbaum died of wounds in Field Hospital No 5 the next day. As both the date and location of the battle tally with the Russian encounter, there is every reason to believe that Orlov and his fellow aviators gained a victory on 13 May.

Two months prior to this mission, Orlov had received his first officer's award, the Order of St Anne 4th Class 'for bravery'. By Order No 409, issued by the Supreme Commander-in-Chief on 19 May, he was awarded the title of military pilot for services in battle. Orlov was subsequently decorated with the Order of St Stanislav 3rd Class with Crossed Swords and Bow and the Order of St Vladimir 4th Class with Crossed Swords and Bow.

In September he was sent to the aircraft works in Petrograd and Moscow to receive new aircraft for the Aviation Detachment, returning to the 1st Army AO in October.

On 17 November Orlov was concussed by the bursting of an anti-aircraft shell during a reconnaissance flight. This episode was later described in the citation awarding Orlov the Order of St George. On 21 November he was transferred to the newly formed 7th AD, and on 10 December he was sent to the Odessa Flying School for training on the Nieuport fighter. Here, Orlov learned that he had been awarded the Order of St George 4th Class and given the rank of Podporuchik.

In the spring of 1916 fighter aviation units were created in the Russian Army, Order No 300 of the staff of the Supreme Commander-in-Chief, dated 5 March 1916, initiating the formation of fighter Aviation Detachments. Orlov was sent to the 3rd Aviation Company in Kiev to form the 7th AOI as a unit of the 7th AD. On 30 March the 7th AOI received three two-seat Sikorsky S-16 fighters (s/ns 201, 202 and 204), followed by three Vickers machine guns two days later. The guns were to be mounted on the S-16s and fitted with synchronising gear designed in 1915 by Lieutenant Flota (naval Lieutenant) George Lavrov to enable them to fire through the propeller disc. In addition, Moska-Bystritsky MBbis s/n 2 and a handful of Nieuport 9 and 10 two-seat scouts were also supplied to the squadron from April.

On the 9 April the 7th AOI left for the Southwestern Front, where it would be commanded by the 7th Army staff. A suitable field next to the village of Khmelevka became the unit's first aerodrome. On 15 April the first combat flight was made, when unit CO Podporuchik Orlov and his observer Kornet Lipsky took off in an S-16 to provide aerial cover for the airfield. Two days later the squadron commenced offensive operations, patrolling the Khmelevka-Yanov-Lyaskovtse-Dobropole sector.

Italian-designed and Russian-built, the Moska-Bystritsky MBbis had a Lewis gun mounted at an angle so that it would shoot over the propeller due to its lack of synchronisation gear. As shown in this photograph, the aircraft was constructed in such a way that it could be easily transported by rail

The first air combat took place on 20 April when Praporshchik Matveevich pursued and attacked an enemy two-seat reconnaissance aircraft. However, the enemy observer's return fire hit Matveevich's machine and he had to break off the chase and head home.

On 26 May Podporuchik Orlov gained a victory. That day he took off twice from Travny airfield in MBbis s/n 7 at 1805 hrs and 1930 hrs to pursue enemy aeroplanes. During the second sortie Orlov, flying at 3150 m (10,300 ft), spotted an Austro-Hungarian Lloyd C II. He attacked this machine from an altitude of 2500 m (8200 ft), pursuing the two-seater from Czortkow to the enemy-occupied village of Petlikovtse-Stare. Orlov killed the observer and wounded the pilot, and the aeroplane crashed into a forest near Petlikovtse-Stare. In his report Orlov wrote that, after his attacks, the C II had fled westward. And, although it fell behind the enemy trenches, the victory was credited to him as Russian troops confirmed that they had seen the biplane crash. For this success Orlov was awarded the Gold Sword for Bravery (Order of the Army and the Navy) on 10 April 1917.

Austrian archives suggest that Orlov probably shot down C II 42.21 of *Flik* 9, which was shot down in a fight with a Russian single-seat fighter while it was bombing transport near Czortkow. The observer, Ltn#d R Walter Schmidt, was seriously wounded, as was the pilot, Karl Rumiha. However, he managed to land the badly damaged aircraft with its dead engine behind the Austrian trenches, not far from Osovets. Sixty bullet holes were found in the aircraft.

The wreckage of Aviatik B III 33.30 of *Flik* 27, shot down by Orlov on 13 June 1916. The wounded crew, pilot Zgf Friedrich Schallinger and observer Fähnrich d R Gustav Wängler, were captured after making a forced landing near Burkanovsky Forest

According to 7th AOI records regarding aircraft shot down between 16 April 1916 and 24 July 1917, on 13 June 1916 Orlov (in Nieuport 10 N205) and Praporshchik Yanchenko shot down an enemy aircraft near Burkanovsky Forest. However, a *communiqué* from the staff of the Supreme Commander-in-Chief dated 14 June 1916 confirms that there was only one Russian participant in this encounter;

'On 13 June our pilot Podporuchik Orlov overtook the enemy pilot at a height of 2400 m [7900 ft], engaged him in combat and forced him to descend in a steep bank near Podhaice village.'

Austrian archives record that Aviatik B III 33.30 of *Flik* 27 was lost on that date. The wounded crew, pilot Zgf Friedrich Schallinger and observer Fähnrich d R Gustav Wängler, were captured after making a forced landing.

On 3 September the 7th AOI redeployed to a new airfield near Vychulki Farm. At 0920 hrs on 22 September Orlov and Yanchenko took off in two Nieuport Bébés to pursue an enemy aeroplane. Orlov was flying Nieuport 21 N1514, armed with a Lewis machine gun, and Yanchenko was in Nieuport 11 N1302. Orlov attacked from the rear. Having blocked the enemy pilot's route to Brzeżany, Yanchenko attacked it, firing tracer rounds. The Russian pilots testified;

Famous French ace Georges Guynemer with Orlov (right) near a SPAD VII of *Escadrille* N3 in France. On 24 January 1917 Orlov shot down an enemy aeroplane, which made an emergency landing to the north of Fresnoy village, near the city of Roye in the Somme sector of the front. He was almost certainly flying a SPAD VII from N3, and for this victory he was awarded the French *Croix de Guerre* with palm (*Christophe Cony*)

'We saw the enemy aeroplane suddenly begin to fall, and a stream of black smoke was seen. At that moment we were attacked by another enemy aeroplane, which we fired on, forcing it to fly away to its base.'

Further details of this combat are found in Communiqué No 5 of the staff of the Supreme Commander-in-Chief, dated 24 September 1916, which reported;

'In the Złota Lipa River region six air combats took place. Podporuchik Orlov and Praporshchik Yanchenko, pursuing an enemy aeroplane, successfully set it on fire with tracer bullets. The enemy aeroplane descended, enveloped in smoke.'

Another report gives a somewhat different account of the end of the fight, stating 'after being hit by machine gun fire the enemy fell in flames in the region of Brzeżany'. As yet, no information has been found in Austrian or German archives to confirm this victory.

In November 1916 Orlov went to France, and Observer Kapitan Medel was appointed temporary commander of the 7th AOI. It took a long time to get from Murmansk to Brest, the voyage lasting several weeks. Along with pilots I G Kezhun, E N Kruten, A N Sveshnikov, S K Shebalin and others, Orlov was sent to the Western Front to gain combat experience. He completed a course of training in the famous Stork squadron (*Escadrille* N3), after which he was sent out on operational patrols. French historian Christophe Cony records that at 1145 hrs on 24 January 1917, Orlov shot down an enemy aeroplane, which made an emergency landing to the north of Fresnoy village, near the city of Roye in the Somme sector of the front. He was probably flying a SPAD VII, and for this victory he was awarded the French *Croix de Guerre* with palm.

At the end of January six pilots, including Orlov, returned to Russia, while the remainder went to London to continue their training. On 7 March Orlov returned to Petrograd, where the February Revolution had recently taken place. Crowded political meetings, drunken soldiers and the revolutionary euphoria were not to his taste. Having visited the Air Fleet Department, where he submitted a report about his foreign mission, Orlov returned to the front.

Before rejoining his squadron he had a nine-page brochure printed, entitled *Ways of Conducting an Air Combat*. It was published that year by the Aviation and Aeronautics Field Department Bureau. In his small work devoted to fighter tactics, Orlov summarised the combat experience he had gained mainly in France during his training course. Sixteen main points necessary for successful air combat are described, and they include the attack from above and out of the sun with a height advantage of 500-1000 m (1600-3300 ft) when an enemy least expects it, and the diving attack perpendicular to the opponent's direction of flight. Here is an extract;

'Having flown below the enemy aeroplane, begin to make a loop and end it with a roll, levelling out in close proximity under your opponent's tail. When below the enemy machine, choose a moment to dive away, then again gain altitude and fire a burst from your machine gun. Having stopped shooting, dive, without waiting for the result, to avoid a collision.'

Orlov wrote that this method of attack was most reliable, and the least dangerous, saying it had been recommended to him by legendary aces Georges Guynemer and Alfred Heurtaux of *Escadrille* N3. He noted that he had successfully put it into practice when he shot down the enemy

A SPAD VII of *Escadrille* N3, with whom Orlov underwent training courses and then flew operational patrols

The cover of Orlov's nine-page booklet entitled *Ways of Conducting an Air Combat – Necessary General Information*. It was published that year by the Aviation and Aeronautics Field Department Bureau. In his small work devoted to fighter tactics, Orlov summarised the combat experience he had gained mainly in France during his training course

ПРІЕМЫ ВЕДЕНІЯ

ВОЗДУШНАГО БОЯ.

ОБЩІЯ НЕОБХОДИМЫЯ СВѢДѢНІЯ.

Изданіе Канцеляріи Полевого Управленія
авіаціи и воздухоплаванія
при Штабѣ Верховнаго Главнокомандующаго.

An official portrait of Ivan Aleksandrovich Orlov, taken during 1917

aeroplane near Roye on 24 January. Orlov recommended two ways of escape when enemy fighters attacked from the rear – go into a spin, or if many fighters attacked you, go into a flat spin. He had had to break off the fight on the 24th when he was targeted by two Halberstadt fighters, using the spinning method to escape.

Having arrived at the front without delay, Orlov joined in combat operations. In April he took part in 13 sorties, flying from an airfield situated near Markovtse. The 7th AOI pilots flew combat missions on the Monasterzyska-Kałusz-Stanisławów-Maidany-Bohorodczany sector of the front.

During a patrol on 8 April Orlov and Makijonek sighted an enemy aeroplane in the region of Kolodziewka. Orlov (in Nieuport 11 N679) attacked and either killed or wounded the observer, who ceased returning fire. The Russian was then himself attacked by another enemy aircraft, and he joined battle with it. Makijonek also entered the fray over Stanisławów, forcing the enemy pilot to descend near Maidan. After that the Russian aviators were attacked by a third enemy machine and had to make their escape, as their ammunition was spent.

On 9 May 7th AOI commander Podporuchik Orlov, again in N1679, took off to patrol along the route Stanisławów-Iezupol-Halich. Over the village of Rybno he spotted a hostile Albatros flying towards the Russian positions, attacked it and forced it to descend near Mysluzh village. Resuming his patrol, Orlov saw two more enemy aircraft, one of which was large and armed with two machine guns. He attacked this aircraft over Prisup and the enemy pilot in turn did his best to engage him. After Orlov's second attack his opponent made an emergency landing on the western slope of Russian-occupied Height 829, to the south of Yasen. There is every reason to believe that Orlov had shot down a two-seat Albatros scout of *Flieger Abteilung (Artillerie) 242*. Both crew members were captured.

The command of the 7th AD appreciated Orlov's abilities as a fighter pilot, and regarded him as a brave and persistent officer and a perfect commander for the detachment. However, this did not help him gain promotion. Orlov had been given the rank of Podporuchik in November 1915, and in June 1917 he was still awaiting his next promotion.

At the start of that month the 7th AOI was based at Kozova airfield, but is soon moved to Vikturovka so as to cover the Plotych-Brzeżany-Khinovize-Kuropatniki-Suhov sector of the front. The 7th AOI numbered just six pilots and eight Nieuport fighters at this time, and it undertook intensive combat operations, including, in addition to air combat, reconnaissance, photography, escorting Voisin artillery spotters and bombing. Orlov flew French-built Nieuport 11 N1679 throughout this period, despite the fact that the aircraft was virtually worn out following seven months of service with the squadron.

In June Orlov made 13 combat flights. On the 3rd he took off in Nieuport 10 N702 with observer Shtabs-Kapitan Alexey Orlov and dropped three bombs on a train of carts concentrated near Maidanskaya Buda. On 7 June Orlov and Yanchenko were on patrol when they came across five enemy aircraft, two of which joined them in battle. In his report Orlov wrote that one of the enemy pilots had glided down behind his own trench lines near Lesniki village. On the 13th Orlov lent a timely

Albatros (Oeffag) D II 53.11 of *Flik* 25, based in the Galicia region during the summer of 1917. It was probably two fighters of this type that shot down Orlov's Nieuport 23 on 17 June, killing the ace. The lower right wing of the scout was seen to break and tear away moments after the engagement had ended, the fighter plunging to the ground from 3000 m (10,000 ft) and crashing among Russian troops near the first line of trenches to the west of Kozova (*Tomasz Kopanski*)

helping hand to his comrade when an enemy aeroplane tried to attack Yanchenko from behind. Orlov attacked the enemy pilot, who avoided action and flew away behind the lines. Orlov had to break off the chase because of a ruptured bullet case and the subsequent failure of his machine gun.

Four days later Detachment Commander Podporuchik Ivan Orlov was killed in combat. His first flight that day was a patrol and reconnaissance in N702, again with observer Aleksey Orlov. Near Rohatyn-Brzeżany they attacked enemy aeroplanes and drove them off to the rear. On his next flight Orlov took off at 2000 hrs in new Nieuport 23 N2788, armed with a Vickers machine gun, for a patrol over the Kozova- Brzeżany region. Over the latter town he was attacked by two enemy fighters, and moments after the engagement had ended the Nieuport's lower right wing broke and tore away. The fighter plunged to the ground from 3000 m (10,000 ft), crashing among Russian troops near the first line of trenches to the west of Kozova, tragically ending the life of an outstanding pilot.

Orlov's death might well have been caused by the insecure fastening of the lower wings – a serious structural defect that plagued a large number of Nieuport sesquiplane fighters. Failure or rupture of the lower wings owing to overloading while manoeuvring caused repeated crashes.

On 20 June the body of pilot Ivan Orlov was sent for burial in Tsarskoe Selo, not far from Petrograd. His comrade observer, Shtabs-Kapitan Alexey Orlov, escorted the coffin.

Yuri Gilsher

Yuri Gilsher was born on 14 November 1894 in Moscow, his father being a gentleman by birth. Yuri finished his education at the Moscow Alexeyevskoye Commercial School, and when World War 1 commenced he volunteered for military service. On 30 November 1914 Gilsher began his training with a short-term course at the Nikolaevsky Cavalry School in St Petersburg, which he completed on 1 June 1915 with the rank of Praporshchik.

As he was a student of the cavalry school he requested a transfer to aviation, and on 3 June was sent to Gatchina Military Flying School. After graduation on 8 October he was assigned to the 4th KAO, being given the title of military pilot nine days later. The formation of the 4th KAO was soon completed, and on 27 October it departed for the front. On 7 November, as a result of an accident while starting an engine, Gilsher fractured both bones in his right forearm and was evacuated.

Gilsher was subsequently sent to the Moscow Dux aircraft factory, where he found employment checking that spare parts manufactured for military aircraft were fit for use. Having recovered from his injury, Gilsher requested a transfer to the Odessa Flying School to learn to fly on the latest aircraft type – fighters – in February 1916. On 8 March he was assigned to the newly formed 7th AOI.

Later that same month the unit arrived in the Tarnopol region of the front. The squadron's equipment included three new S-16 fighters, created by well-known Russian aircraft designer Igor Sikorsky. These multi-purpose two-seat biplanes were armed with a synchronised Vickers machine gun. In addition to the S-16s, the unit also had Moska-Bystritsky MB s/n 2 and a small number of Nieuport 9 and 10 two-seaters.

A Sikorsky S-16 multi-purpose two-seat fighter/reconnaissance biplane, fitted with a synchronised Vickers gun. These Russian designed and built machines were some of the first aircraft issued to 7th AOI upon its formation in March 1916

On 30 March Gilsher was promoted to the rank of Kornet.

In April the 7th AOI was based at an airfield in Khmelevka village, and its pilots were under the command of the Southwestern Front 7th Army staff. They patrolled the Yanov-Khmelevka-Lyaskovtse-Dobropole sector of the front, Gilsher performing his first combat sorties on 16 April – he would undertake four patrols and one reconnaissance mission that month.

At 1900 hrs on 27 April Gilsher, with observer Praporshchik Kvasnikov in the rear cockpit, took off in S-16 s/n 201 to pursue an enemy Aviatik B III two-seater. The machine was found over Burkanov village, successfully attacked at 2500 m (8200 ft) and shot down. According to Austrian records, on that day Zgf Alexander Galbavy and observer Kdt d R Julius Horak of *Flik* 20, in Aviatik B III 33.02, were forced to land five kilometres (three miles) behind the Russian trenches after an engagement that resulted in their engine being damaged. The downed airmen tried to burn the aeroplane, but Russian cavalrymen arrived in time to prevent it, and the captive pilots were taken on horseback to the nearest staff headquarters. For this successful combat Gilsher and Kvasnikov were awarded the Order of St Vladimir 4th Class with Swords and Bow.

Having despatched the Aviatik, the Russians turned for home, but at a height of 1200 m (4000 ft) over the airfield their S-16 went out of control, entered a spin and crash-landed. It transpired that the port elevator had jammed in the lowered position, this accident revealing a serious design fault in the S-16's control system – its port and starboard elevators were not interconnected. Miraculously, both men were alive but badly injured, especially Kornet Gilsher, whose left leg and foot were crushed. Once he had been removed from the tangled debris he was sent to a field hospital, where his left foot was amputated.

Gilsher seemingly had no chance of flying again, but after being discharged from the hospital he fought hard to return to aviation. At the end of October 1916 the Head of the Military Air Fleet Department helped the young pilot return to the front. On 30 October Kornet Gilsher was re-enlisted as a military pilot in the 7th AOI. He subsequently spent a lot of time in the cockpit of a Nieuport fighter during ground

**An informal portrait of five-victory
ace Praporshchik Yury Gilsher of the
7th AOI in 1917**

training, and then performed a series of short flights over the airfield. Gradually, Gilsher mastered piloting the aircraft using his prosthetic left foot.

His first combat flight for more than six months took place on 9 November, when he and observer Shtabs-Kapitan Mikhail Mendel undertook visual reconnaissance and aerial photography of enemy positions. Under heavy anti-aircraft fire, Gilsher calmly flew over the second line of trenches, enabling his observer to take good photographs and spot a new enemy artillery battery. That same day he made another flight of an hour-and-a-half's duration in pursuit of a hostile aeroplane, but the German pilot flew away over the frontline. Gilsher quickly got used to the routine of combat flying, escorting reconnaissance aircraft, patrolling the 7th AOI's sector of the front and pursuing enemy aircraft.

He claimed his second aerial success on 31 March 1917 when he and two squadronmates attacked two enemy aircraft – Gilsher was flying French-built Nieuport 21 N1872 at the time. After a ten-minute combat Poruchik Makijonek and Praporshchik Yanchenko shot down an enemy aircraft, which burst into flames and fell into the forest west of Maidanska Buda. Kornet Gilsher and Praporshchik Yanchenko attacked the second aeroplane, and after a violent fight this machine was also shot down. Streaming black smoke, it disappeared in the direction of Posech village. Their victim was a two-seat reconnaissance aircraft from *Flik* 7, its observer, Ltn Szeliga, being wounded in both legs. Pilot Zgf Klefac somehow managed to return home and land the badly damaged machine.

With the coming of warm summer days air combat resumed with renewed vigour. Indeed, the 7th AOI pilots now performed several flights a day. During the morning of 2 May Gilsher was patrolling the region of Halych-Jezupol-Użcie-Zielone when he saw a hostile aircraft at 3880 m (12,725 ft) over Bolshovtsy. The observer of the Austro-Hungarian Oeffag C II fired first, eventually exhausting his ammunition as he vainly attempted to shoot Gilsher down – he even resorted to firing at him with his signal pistol. The observer then stopped shooting, and Gilsher saw him raise his hands several times as a sign of surrender and point at the ground. However, the Russian pressed home his attack and the C II fell close to Boushuv village, south of Bolshovtsy. It was later destroyed on the ground by Russian artillery. Austrian archives record that the aircraft was C II 52.52 from *Flik* 25. The observer, Oblt i d R Julius Hochenegg, was killed, but pilot Zgf Pius Moosbrugger survived.

Gilsher was awarded the Order of St George 4th Class, 7th Army Order No 670 of 15 May 1917, the citation for the decoration noting, 'For the deed on 2 May 1917, when, having met a hostile aeroplane, he shot it down in an air fight. The machine fell near Boushuv village'. Shortly afterwards, by 7th Army Order No 705 of 20 May 1917, Gilsher was awarded the Order of St Anne 4th Class with the legend 'For Bravery'.

Now an experienced fighter pilot, Gilsher frequently stood in for the detachment commander when the latter was absent – he was a promising candidate for the post of commander. In early June the command wanted to appoint him CO of the 4th AOI in place of Sotnik (Cossack Lieutenant)

Fedor Zverev, who was being sent to a new post in the rear. Military pilot Shtabs-Kapitan Vyacheslav Baranov, commanding the 7th AD, which included the 7th AOI, rated his comrade highly;

'Kornet Gilsher is an excellent combat pilot, resolute, brave, cool. An aviation enthusiast. When replacing the squadron commander he maintained discipline and order. Of high moral qualities, he seriously and conscientiously fulfils the assigned tasks. Outstanding. I regard him as a worthy candidate for the post of a detachment commander.'

However, Gilsher did not leave his squadron for the new post, as events at the front changed the situation. On 22 June the 7th AOI commander, Podporuchik Ivan Orlov, perished in an unequal combat, and Gilsher was appointed in his place. The command had no reason to doubt the choice, as shortly before his death Orlov had also given Gilsher a brilliant testimonial.

In June the offensive by Russian troops on the Southwestern Front intensified the activity of the enemy's aviation units, which enjoyed quantitative and qualitative advantages over their counterparts in the Imperial Military Air Fleet. Throughout the month pilots from the 7th AOI participated in intense aerial combat, making several flights a day. In a letter to his sister, Kornet Gilsher described the everyday life of his squadron during the early summer of 1917;

'We get up at 0800 hrs and run to the airfield to check the machines and try their motors and machine guns. If everything is all right we drag the machines to a takeoff position, and then we sit down on a bench and listen. One can pick up the sound of an aeroplane by ear sooner than

Gilsher is seen here sitting on the ski-equipped undercarriage of a Nieuport 10 with his dog, surrounded by fellow pilots from the 7th AOI

one can see it. Our comrade observers pass by in their huge heavy machines. They take off and circle slowly to pick up speed, then they depart in the direction of the front. After a while one can see the Germans put them under artillery fire – the machines are very often tangled in black smoke.

'When white puffs of smoke appear on the horizon, it means our artillery has put a German aeroplane under fire, and we have to ascend. We get into our "Bébés" fast, take off and start the battle. Last time I was just 80 m [250 ft] behind a German, but my machine gun jammed and I hardly escaped his bullets. The cracking of enemy machine guns is very unpleasant.'

Enemy aircraft were engaged every day, and Gilsher's worn-out Nieuport 11 was not as safe as it had once been. The fighter's Le Rhône was now down on power, the bracing wires were creaking under the load and the solitary Lewis gun often misfired. Before each flight Gilsher and his mechanic checked and adjusted the whole aeroplane. There was a shortage of all aircraft types at the front, but especially fighters. However, in the hands of the experienced pilots of the 7th KAO the old machines were formidable weapons.

Kornet Gilsher proved this once again on 4 July when, in a combat at 1100 hrs he shot down an enemy aeroplane over Posukhov while flying Nieuport 11 N1679. After his attack the hostile scout went down almost vertically and crashed in enemy territory to the southwest of Posukhov. The wreckage of the aircraft was destroyed on the ground by Russian artillery. The *Casualty List of German Air Forces during the World War 1* records that on 4 July 1917, pilot Gefr Arno Naumann perished in the region of Brzeżany. The fate of his observer is unknown.

Kornet Gilsher was awarded the Gold Sword for Bravery in 7th Army Order No 1888 of 21 November 1917, which stated, 'On 4 July 1917, during pursuit of an enemy aircraft over Posukhov village, he shot it down, and on 7 July 1917 he became engaged in an unequal battle with seven fighters, in which he perished'.

On 7 July Gilsher, together with Praporshchik Yanchenko, took off at 2000 hrs to repulse an attack by a hostile squadron intent on bombing Tarnopol. During their first attack the Russian pilots shot down an enemy two-seater, which descended steeply. Gilsher then went after another enemy machine, approaching it from behind and closing to 70 m (75 yd). Yanchenko attacked the same aeroplane from above and to the right. Gilsher's Nieuport 21 (N2451) came under fire from the enemy observer, and tracer bullets riddled the aircraft's fuselage. Suddenly the engine tore away from the airframe and flew off. The Nieuport's wings then folded up and the fighter fell away and crashed. With difficulty, Yanchenko shook off the remaining enemy aircraft and landed at the scene of the crash. He removed Gilsher's body from the wreckage and had it sent to Tarnopol. The veteran aviator was later buried in Buchach (Galicia).

An order issued by the 7th AOI, dated 7 July 1917, stated, in part;

'In the person of Kornet Gilsher the detachment lost its second commander, who carried out his duty for his Fatherland piously, heroically and with moral intelligence. Let the deeds of this military pilot serve as an example to all fighting men of boundless devotion to Russia.'

ACES OF THE 9th AOI

Grigory Suk

Grigory Suk was born on 29 November 1896 on the Rassudovo Estate near Moscow. His father was a hereditary honorary citizen of Moscow. After graduating from Moscow Classical School, Suk became a student at the Moscow Imperial Practical Academy as he trained to become an architect. However, the outbreak of war abruptly changed his plans.

On 23 July 1914 Suk entered military service as a volunteer, young soldiers being trained in the Cuirassiers' barracks near Petrograd. He soon requested a transfer to serve in the air arm, and on 27 May 1915 was assigned to the Gatchina Flying School. However, it was not until early July that Suk managed to begin his studies, starting with an engine class. Making his first training flights a month later, Suk passed the test for the title of military pilot on a Farman F 16 on 12 January 1916.

In February that year Suk was assigned to the 26th KAO, joining the unit on 15 March. Equipped with Voisin L and LA biplanes, the 26th was part of the 9th AD, which was in turn attached to the 9th Army on the Southwestern Front. Suk fought with the 26th KAO until June 1916, and during that period the young pilot was awarded the soldier's Crosses of St George in all four Classes and given the rank of Starshyi Unter-Officer for performing a series of successful reconnaissance missions.

Suk also confronted the enemy in the air whilst with the 26th, the Order awarding him the soldier's St George Cross 4th Class stating that it was bestowed upon him 'for important reconnaissance information and a fight with an enemy Albatros'. In another Order from the 9th Army staff regarding his award of the soldier's St George Cross 3rd Class, the following information about his first successful combat appears in the paperwork generated for the decoration;

'On 19 May 1916, after photographing positions in the Chernelitsa-Potochiska-Horodenka-Zalischyky region and returning from the reconnaissance mission, he met with an enemy aircraft over Shchukino village. Joining battle with it, he approached to 50 m [55 yd] distance. He damaged it with machine gun fire, forcing it to glide with its engine stopped. The Albatros fell among the enemy's trenches.'

Mladshy Unter-Officer Suk was flying Voisin V979, and his observer was Shtabs-Rotmistr Andrey Bode.

On 21 June Grigory Suk was sent to Moscow Military Flying School to train on fighters. He was then assigned to the 9th AOI and posted to the Rumanian Front. This unit was formed following the Russian Army's successful offensive on the Southwestern Front, which saw the

Mladshy Unter-Officer Grigory Suk in May 1916, straddling the rear cockpit of a Nieuport 10 – the type of aircraft in which he subsequently began his career as a fighter pilot with the 9th AOI. On his field jacket shines his first decoration, the soldier's Order of St George 4th Class. Suk had received this award 'for important reconnaissance information and a fight with an enemy Albatros' whilst flying Voisin L and LA biplanes with the 26th KAO between March and June 1916

Austro-Hungarian Empire brought to the brink of defeat. Rumania decided to join the Entente, but owing to its army's extremely poor state of readiness, it suffered a defeat, forcing Russian troops to rescue its hapless ally.

During September-October 1916 Grigory Suk made 19 operational flights. For battle honours he was promoted to the rank of Praporshchik (Imperial Order No 1676 of 14 October). Suk's service with the 9th AOI commenced with him making reconnaissance flights in Nieuport 10 N714, after which he flew patrols in Nieuport 11 N1109. From February 1917 the young pilot mastered Morane-Saulnier Type I MS742.

The combat activities of pilots on both sides intensified when spring brought better weather. On 13 March 1917 Suk gained his second victory whilst flying MS742 on a patrol in the region of Sżuceşti-Ocna-Bacżu. From an altitude of 4600 m (15,000 ft) he saw a hostile biplane flying from Kéizul to Kézdi-Vàsárhely at 3600 m (11,800 ft). Suk dived and attacked the enemy machine (a Hansa-Brandenburg C I), opening fire at a range of 300 m (330 yd) and continuing to fire until there was only 20 m (22 yd) between them. The damaged enemy aircraft began to turn and descend westwards. Making a high-speed dive, Suk turned and attacked the C I on a collision course. His bullets probably hit the biplane's engine, as it began a rapid descent, but he lost sight of the falling aircraft and returned to his airfield.

Russian troops confirmed the victory and Austro-Hungarian records show that C I 67.24 of *Flik* 40 made a forced landing in the Bistriża region on 26 March. Its crew, pilot Kpl Kenedy and observer Ltn d R Duller, were slightly injured. This was probably the aircraft shot down by Suk.

That same day the 9th AOI moved to Borzeżti airfield, pilots patrolling the Onceşti-Pralea-Oituz-Ocna sector of the front from here and often engaging hostile scouts in combat. On 17 April Suk took off to escort a Voisin of the 28th KAO that was to photograph the enemy's positions in the region of Ocna-Čik Szereda. During the mission two enemy aircraft tried to disrupt the Voisin whilst it was conducting its photo passes, but Praporshchik Suk attacked them and drove them away.

During June-July 1917 the pilots of the 9th AD of the Rumanian Front 9th Army fought under great stress, making several sorties per day. Suk gained his next victory on 27 July while flying Nieuport 21 N1719 over Ocna. According to Austrian records, a crew from *Flik* 44 were conducting aerial spotting in Oeffag C III 52.63 on the route Kézdi-Vàsárhely-Herastru-Par Lesunta when the aircraft was shot down by an enemy aeroplane. Pilot Zgf Adolf Rabl was killed in the air, but observer Oblt i d R Franz Xaver Schlarbaum managed to land the damaged C III in Rumanian territory. The observer eventually returned from Russian captivity on 9 April 1918.

At the end of July the 9th AOI was transferred to the airfield near the city of Fżlticeni, in northern Rumania, where the detachment received new machines. In the second half of August Suk exchanged Nieuport 21 N1719 for British-built Vickers FB 19 No 12.

On 20 August, during his second operational flight that day, Suk, at the controls of the FB 19, pursued an enemy Hansa-Brandenburg C I that had appeared over the Suceava River. Climbing to a height of 4600 m (15,000 ft), he and Podporuchik Loiko in Nieuport 17 N1448 attacked the enemy machine from behind over the village of Islovăż. Loiko

Morane-Saulnier Type I MS742 was delivered to the 9th AOI on 6 February 1917, where it was armed with a synchronised Vickers machine gun. On 13 March Suk forced down a Hansa-Brandenburg C I while at the controls of this machine. Deemed to be worn out by May, the monoplane fighter was placed in storage in the 6th Aviation Park

was slightly higher than the C I, and Suk somewhat below the enemy aircraft. They opened fire at a range of 150 m (160 yd), and continued firing until they were 20 m (22 yd) from the C I. The enemy observer first fired at Loiko's aeroplane and then at Suk, after which his pilot turned in the direction of Rădăuţi and began to descend.

Loiko had to break off, as his gun had jammed, but Suk again attacked and the observer returned fire. The hostile aeroplane went into a steep dive and crashed in the Suceava River valley between Rădăuţi and Volovăţ. Suk had probably shot down pilot Kpl Julius Jahn of *Flik* 36 and observer Ltn d R Thaddeus Wereszynski of *Flik* 39, whose aircraft, C I 67.31, was shot down in the Russian Army's rear at that time.

On almost all of their flights the Russian pilots encountered anti-aircraft fire. On 26 August shell splinters broke the air-pressure pump of Suk's aeroplane and he had to abandon the flight. Machine gun failures were also frequent. On 30 August three pilots, Podporuchik Loiko in Nieuport 17 N1448, Praporshchik Suk in Vickers FB 19 No 12 and Unter-Officer Sapozhnikov in Nieuport 17 N1445, took off to patrol the Arbore-Rădăuţi-Hadikfalva sector. Over Islovăž village they simultaneously attacked an enemy aeroplane from behind, and the machine dived towards Rădăuţi, smoking heavily until it reached the ground. The attacks had commenced at an altitude of 3200 m (10,500 ft) and continued down to 1700 m (5500 ft).

Austrian documents record that pilot, Oblt i d R Georg Altadonna, and observer, Oblt Adalbert Kuncze, of *Flik* 44 were returning from a reconnaissance mission when their aircraft was attacked over Scherbautz by Russian aeroplanes. The engine was damaged and the pilot was wounded in the neck, but he managed to force-land behind the Austrian trenches near Rădăuţi. The aircraft type is unknown.

Early in September the 9th AOI received SPAD VII fighters, Suk being issued with S1440. The new aircraft was far superior to the other fighter

Vickers FB 19 fighters of the 9th AOI at Fälticeni airfield on the Rumanian Front in August 1917. Although only a small number of these machines were supplied to the Russians, and their frontline service was limited to barely two months, Grigory Suk claimed his fourth and fifth victories while flying FB 19 No 12

Praporshchik Suk in the autumn of 1917. He had claimed eight victories by the time he was killed in a flying accident on 15 November that year

types then equipping Russian squadrons, and as a rule the best pilots were the first to get them. Suk was one of them, his commander, Podporuchik Loiko, giving him the following testimonial;

'An excellent pilot, he can perform combat missions brilliantly in difficult conditions. He loves his occupation, is dutiful and accurate, but he lacks experience, as he has only recently been promoted to officer rank, and could not occupy responsible posts. In service and private life he keeps himself well, and may be a worthy officer.'

Information regarding the flights made by Suk in September is almost non-existent, but there is much more about his flights in October. A Rumanian command communiqué dated 1 October 1917 records that at about 1200 hrs Praporshchik Suk of the 9th AOI shot down a German fighter on his first attack, and it had fallen behind Russian trenches near Gura Solcăi, southeast of Rădăuţi. The enemy aircraft was destroyed and its pilot killed. Suk, who had taken off to patrol the Seret-Hadikfalva-Slobozia-Todireşti region, later wrote;

'While flying at a height of 3600 m (11,800 ft), I saw above me an enemy aircraft flying from Rădăuţi to Todireşti. I climbed to 4200 m (13,800 ft), and when the enemy machine flew across our positions I overtook him over Slobozia. I looped behind his tail, dived and attacked the enemy in a vertical climb.'

Suk fired 45 bullets from point-blank range, killing his opponent and damaging his aeroplane, which banked away and began falling in a flat spin with its engine running. Its wings were quickly torn away and the fuselage crashed near Slobozia. Fragments of the aircraft and the body of its Austrian pilot-sergeant were delivered to the squadron. The battered fuselage was seen to bear the board number 53.20, while the machine was powered by 180 hp Austro-Daimler engine No 18190. The pilot was buried with military honours the next day. Austrian archives record that on 1 October Fw Johann Obeslo of *Flik* 40, flying Albatros D III (Oeffag) 53.20, was shot down during air combat.

Increasingly, enemy pilots tried to avoid engaging with Russian fighters, descending rapidly when attacked so as to gain the protection of numerous anti-aircraft batteries. On 29 October 1917, issue No 50 of the newspaper *The Voice of the Front* reported, 'On 26 October Praporshchik Suk shot down his seventh hostile aeroplane'. During a patrol at 3800 m (12,500 ft), while flying over Suceava-Hadikfalva-Rădăuţi, Suk attacked an enemy aircraft over Deutsch şi Satul Mare. After his third attack from below and behind, the enemy machine began descending steeply before entering a flat spin and falling away enveloped in smoke. It crash-landed to the north of Rădăuţi, but confirmation of the victory has not been found in German or Austrian archives.

On 28 October Suk took off in SPAD VII S1440 to conduct aerial reconnaissance of the railway line between Rădăuţi, Seletin and Izvor. However, he failed to carry out this task as he became engaged in prolonged combat with three enemy aircraft that had intercepted him over Streja. Suk attacked the nearest aircraft, which quickly lost height and fled for the safety of its own airfield. He then attacked the second machine, but without success. Getting onto the tail of the third enemy aircraft over Solca, he pursued it to Volovăţ, where, after his sixth attack, he lost sight of it.

Austrian archives record that the crew, pilot Kpl Milan Alterow and observer Oblt i d R Jgnaz Patch, both of *Flik* 49, were involved in a fight with a Russian SPAD fighter. Patch was wounded in the left shoulder, and their aeroplane, Hansa-Brandenburg C I 269.49, received 16 holes in the engine, wings and struts. The pilot managed to land his damaged aircraft in friendly territory near Rădăuți.

This C I proved to be Praporshchik Suk's last victory. On 15 November, 'returning from a combat flight, military pilot Praporshchik Suk made a turn to land on the airfield. His aeroplane stalled, went into a spin and crashed, the pilot being smashed to death'. Three days later 9th Army Order No 672 announced that Grigory Suk had been awarded the Order of St George 4th Class, but it was too late for the Russian hero to receive his decoration.

Vladimir Strzhizhevsky

Vladimir Strzhizhevsky (spelt Strizhevsky in some documents) was born in Mogilev on 13 December 1894 into a family of gentry. A student of Petrograd Polytechnic Institute, he volunteered for the army on 1 October 1914. On 16 July 1915 he graduated from Sevastopol Military Flying School and was assigned to the 16th KAO. For combat merits Strzhizhevsky was awarded the soldier's Cross of St George in all four classes and given the rank of Praporshchik. Following a flying accident in February 1916 he was evacuated to the rear for medical treatment that continued until mid-summer. By an Imperial edict dated 2 August 1916, Strzhizhevsky was awarded the title of military pilot 'for selfless work during the war'. In the autumn of that year he joined the 9th fighter AOI.

Strzhizhevsky had received his first taste of aerial combat during his time with the 16th KAO. On 27 October 1915, with observer Unter-Officer Avchukhov, in Morane-Saulnier Type L MS496, he attacked a captive observation balloon southwest of Vaga. The pair circled over the balloon twice, dropping two bombs and 50 metal darts on it, whereupon the blimp fell to the ground. Another encounter occurred on 7 February 1916, when pilot Praporshchik Strzhizhevsky and observer Praporshchik Eremenko took off in Morane-Saulnier Type L MS507 to reconnoitre Ocna-Yurkuts-Zastavki-Zalischyky-Shchitovtse. Over Zastavki they came across an enemy aeroplane and attacked it. After an exchange of fire the enemy machine descended rapidly and forced-landed near Zalischyky.

Grigory Suk scored his final three victories flying SPAD VII S1440 during October 1917. On 15 November 1917 he stalled the fighter while coming in to land at the completion of a mission, the ace perishing in the subsequent crash. The fighter had accumulated just 25 hours and 50 minutes of flying time prior to being written off

At the beginning of 1917, after a successful offensive by Austro-Hungarian troops, supported by the German armed forces of Field Marshal August von Mackensen, the Rumanian Front disintegrated and almost all the territory of Rumania was occupied. Only along the Danube and Seret Rivers, where Russian reserves, including the 9th Army, were quickly deployed, did it prove possible to halt the offensive. By that time the 9th AOI had moved to Săuceşti airfield, east of Bacău. The unit's pilots became more active when the weather improved in the spring.

On 4 March Strzhizhevsky took off in Nieuport 21 N1719 to patrol in the Comăneşti-Dărmăneşti valley-Oituz river-Ocna region. The pilot later reported, 'I saw an enemy aeroplane over the Oituz River valley. It was 700 m (2300 ft) below me. I dived from above and behind, quickly overtook the enemy, attacked and fired from almost point-blank range'. After the second attack the enemy machine began to descend fast while the observer returned fire. In spite of this, Strzhizhevsky again closed on his opponent from behind and fired. The enemy aeroplane continued its steep descent, and while Strzhizhevsky was recharging his machine gun he lost sight of his prey. Russian troops later confirmed that an enemy aeroplane had fallen in hostile territory close behind the lines. For this deed Strzhizhevsky was decorated with the Order of St Anne 4th Class 'For bravery' (9th Army Order of the day No 309, March 1917).

At 0900 hrs on the morning of 5 April Praporshchiks Grigory Suk and Vladimir Strzhizhevsky of the 9th AOI took off on patrol. They initially saw shell bursts over Oneăti, aimed at two enemy aeroplanes flying in the direction of Adjud. They attacked these machines near Keitsul, the enemy crews flying at 4000 m (13,000 ft) when they noticed the Russian fighters. They immediately turned to the south towards Touoi, but this did not prevent Strzhizhevsky, in N1719, from intercepting them over the upper reaches of the Karikna River. Attacking them from behind, he fired at his opponent from short range and the hostile machine began to descend steeply and fly erratically. The observer was seen to throw something away. Having made a steep banking turn, the aeroplane sideslipped and then levelled off, before again descending towards the enemy positions.

Praporshchik Suk, in Nieuport 11 N1109, attacked another enemy machine that tried to help the first, forcing it to make a descending retreat. Suk saw the enemy aircraft targeted by Strzhizhevsky enter a spin at a height of 700 m (2300 ft) and fall into the forest near Răcoasa.

On 28 April Strzhizhevsky attacked an aeroplane near Bogdăneşti, and it began to smoke heavily before turning towards the enemy lines. Having made a second pass at his target, the aircraft, enveloped in smoke, forced-landed in enemy trenches.

In the summer of 1917 enemy forces massed on the frontline with the intention of inflicting a decisive blow and resolving the problem on the Rumanian Front. This was eminently possible, as Russian troops were now involved in the revolutionary disturbances that were paralysing the army, which meant that they could not provide the necessary defence for this sector of the Eastern Front. Nevertheless, Russian pilots remained true to their oath and flew regularly on combat tasks. The 9th AOI's airfield was only 13 km (eight miles) from the frontline, and consequently its pilots were kept very busy intercepting enemy aeroplanes (in pairs or in groups), carrying out reconnaissance and spotting.

On 17 June Strzhizhevsky gained his next victory. Having climbed to 5200 m (17,000 ft) in Nieuport 17 N1448 to patrol the Ocna-Dărmăneşti region, he saw an enemy Hansa-Brandenburg C I flying over Russian territory heading from the River Usa towards the River Groşeşti. He attacked the aeroplane from behind near Ocna, and after a prolonged engagement shot it down, despite the observer's return fire. After his third attack the C I's radiator and fuel tank were shot through, its propeller began to rotate slower and slower and the aircraft lost height until it crashed to the west of Poiana Uzului, in the valley of the River Usa.

Unable to land near the crash because the ground was unsuitable, Strzhizhevsky flew on to the 25th KAO's airfield and travelled to the crash site by car. The enemy aeroplane, C I 67.54 of *Flik* 39, had fallen behind the trenches of the 8th Company, 750th Infantry Regiment. During the combat Strzhizhevsky had fired 300 bullets at his opponent. The crew, pilot Kpl Adolf Pranger and observer Ltn Otto Hoffmann, was captured. The pilot had been wounded in the shoulder, but the observer was unhurt. For this victory Strzhizhevsky was awarded the Order of St George 4th Class in an Army and Fleet Order issued on 29 June 1917.

On 5 July a flight of three 9th AOI aeroplanes, flown by Podporuchik Loiko and Praporshchiks Strzhizhevsky and Karklin, attacked a Hansa-Brandenburg C I over Comăneşti, whereupon it began emitting smoke and descended steeply. It was impossible to see where the aeroplane fell because of clouds. During the attack Strzhizhevsky was hit by two bullets in his right leg, forcing him to withdraw from the action. This C I proved to be his fifth, and last, victory.

According to Austrian archive records, pilot Fw August Novak and observer Ltn d R Franz von Firtos of *Flik* 39, flying C I 67.52 powered by a 160 hp Daimler engine, were attacked by Nieuport fighters during a long-range reconnaissance along the route Czick-Szereda-Comanesci-Mte Nemere. Firtos was killed and Novak seriously wounded in his arm during the combat, the latter making a forced landing behind friendly artillery positions not far from the hill town of Magyaros. The aircraft was wrecked.

Strzhizhevsky was sent to a hospital for treatment, and he returned to the 9th AOI in late September. The following month he completed just four combat sorties, all in new SPAD VII S1435, after which he was then transferred to the 10th AOI. On 29 October Strzhizhevsky was promoted to Podporuchik. His last wartime decoration was the Order of St Vladimir 4th Class with Swords and Bow (Order of the day of the Rumanian Front No 1121 on 6 November 1917).

After the October Revolution of 1917 and Russia's withdrawal from the war, Strzhizhevsky was mobilised in the Red Army as an aviation specialist and appointed commander of the 1st Voronezh Aviation Group. On 4 November 1918 he fled across the frontline and joined the White Army. During the Civil War Strzhizhevsky served in the White Army and VSYuR (Armed Forces of South Russia) aviation units. On 21 July 1920, for service in battle, he was promoted to the rank of Kapitan. In November 1920 he left the Crimea with Gen Wrangel's troops, abandoning Russia forever. Strzhizhevsky subsequently emigrated to Yugoslavia, where he joined the air arm of the Serb, Croat and Slovene kingdom. He passed away in Belgrade on 22 August 1940 and was buried in the city's new cemetery.

This photograph of Vladimir Strzhizhevsky was taken in the 1930s after he had emigrated to Yugoslavia

Ivan Loiko

Ivan Loiko was born on 24 January 1892 into a petty-bourgeois family in the province of Minsk. Having completed his schooling he entered Alekseevskoe Military School, from where he graduated on 1 October 1914 with the rank of Podporuchik. The following month Loiko was sent to Sevastopol Military Flying School, and on 20 April 1915 he graduated successfully and was given the title of military pilot.

In May of that year he joined the Army in the Field as a junior officer in the 30th KAO. During subsequent combat with this unit he acquired a reputation as an excellent officer and pilot, winning the respect of his comrades and subordinates. The aviation division command planned to make Loiko commander of the 30th KAO, but then changed its decision and appointed him commander of the 9th AOI on 7 July 1916. On 20 August Loiko finished forming the 9th and departed with it to the front.

He had already seen some aerial combat whilst serving with the 30th KAO. On the South Front on 13 October 1915 a German aircraft was observed over Russian positions, and Podporuchik Loiko and Praporshchiks Vinogradov and Alelyukhin set off in pursuit in three Morane-Saulnier Type Ls. They caught up with the two-seater reconnaissance aircraft near Mamaliga Station and fired at it from point-blank range with Mauser pistols and a Madsen machine gun. After their second attack the enemy machine banked and dived vertically towards Rumanian territory. The Russian pilots were unable to locate where it had fallen, however.

On 20 September 1916 Poruchik Loiko and his observer, Kornet Kazansky, in Nieuport 10 N714 attacked and shot down an enemy two-seat reconnaissance aircraft near Vatra Dornei. The aeroplane fell in enemy-held territory, and only a brief squadron report of this combat survives.

On 14 December 1916 Loiko took off in Nieuport 11 N1109 to patrol the Comăneşti-Ocna-Poiana-Oneǎti region. Seeing a Hansa-Brandenburg over Comăneşti, he closed with the aeroplane at an altitude of 3500 m (11,500 ft) to the south of Ocna and attacked it. The enemy observer fired back in short bursts, but then the aircraft descended steeply towards its own lines. Turning back, Loiko noticed another enemy aircraft flying from Ocna to Oneǎti. He made a head-on pass at the two-seater, firing a burst from less than 50 m (55 yd). The enemy pilot tried to fly away towards Oneǎti, reaching a high speed during his descent. Loiko attacked once again from head-on, but after 15 rounds his machine gun failed and he had to make threatening manoeuvres to force his opponent to fly away from the frontline. Loiko reported that both of his foes were two-seater aeroplanes of the Hansa-Brandenburg type, with one fixed machine gun on the upper wing.

Later the same day Loiko took off to intercept an enemy aircraft that had dropped bombs on the 28th KAO's airfield. After a long chase he finally got to within 200 m (220 yd) of his prey at virtually the same height. Again choosing to attack his opponent head-on, Loiko fired approximately 150 rounds, after which his opponent made a steep turn in the direction of the frontline and fled for home.

On 28 April 1917, flying Morane-Saulnier Type I MS732, Loiko attacked one of two hostile aeroplanes over the Şuşiţa River valley. After the fight the enemy machine descended between the Caşin and Putna Rivers to the east of the Rumanian border. Loiko was credited with its demise.

On 5 July a flight of three aeroplanes from the 9th AOI, flown by Loiko (in Nieuport 17 N1448, with which he would claim all his remaining victories), Strzhizhevsky and Karklin, attacked an enemy aircraft in the Comănești region, and after several passes it was shot down. Their victim was Hansa-Brandenburg C I 67.52, crewed by pilot Fw August Novak and observer Ltn d R Franz Firtos of *Flik* 39. The observer was killed during the combat and the wounded pilot made a forced landing behind his own lines, wrecking the aircraft in the process.

While on patrol on 23 August, Poruchik Loiko and Podporuchik Karklin in Nieuport 17 N1443 saw a two-seat reconnaissance aircraft flying from Fălticeni towards Gura Humorului at 4300 m (14,100 ft). They attacked the aeroplane over Botoșani and its observer returned fire as his pilot dived for Rădăuți. The descending aeroplane was attacked for a second time at 2900 m (9500 ft) not far from Teodereăti. Loiko's machine gun jammed and he broke off the chase to free the weapon. Karklin then attacked the enemy aircraft three times alone until his machine gun also failed.

Later, the 29th AK staff reported that an aeroplane had been shot down in Russian lines close to the 1st Infantry Division trenches. The victory was also confirmed in a communiqué from a Rumanian troop command, containing details of combat actions by pilots from 22 to 29 August 1917.

During a patrol in the Gura Humorului-Solca-Rădăuți region the following evening, Loiko noticed an enemy aircraft at 4200 m (13,800 ft) at 1800 hrs. He attacked it near the villages of Arbora and Glit, and after several firing passes the enemy aeroplane glided down and landed near a stud farm on the southern side of Rădăuți. Fifteen minutes later Loiko saw another hostile aircraft over Rădăuți and Hadikfalva, but then lost sight of it after making a single attacking pass. At 1845 hrs over Siret, the Russian pilot saw a third aircraft amid shell bursts and attacked it twice near Hadikfalva. After the second pass the Nieuport's machine gun jammed and Loiko returned to his airfield.

At 1230 hrs on 25 August Loiko saw an enemy reconnaissance aeroplane circling over Arbora and Glit at 3000 m (9800 ft). The Russian attacked, firing 230 rounds, and the pilot made a steep turn towards his lines, gliding with the aeroplane's engine shut down in the direction of Mardzina, where he probably made an emergency landing.

Later that same day Loiko took off again in pursuit of an enemy aeroplane that had appeared over the 9th AOI's airfield. He finally closed on the aircraft over Balcouă at 3300 m (10,800 ft), and as he opened fire the enemy pilot turned first towards Teodereăti and then Hadikfalva and Botoșani. Loiko made two more passes, and after the third attack from behind, to the north of Hadikfalva, the enemy observer ceased firing owing to a malfunctioning machine gun. The stricken aircraft began to descend, and Loiko turned and attacked it for a fourth time. The aeroplane continued to glide earthward until it landed near Unter-Horodniki, beside a small railway station. This engagement had occurred at 1740 hrs, and Loiko had fired 420 rounds during his four attacks.

At 1830 hrs at 2700 m (8900 ft) over Deutsch și Satul Mare, Loiko saw yet another enemy aeroplane and attacked it, together with Praporshchik Suk in Vickers FB 19 No 12. The enemy machine then descended near Rădăuți, at which time Loiko broke off his attack as he had used up all of his ammunition.

On 30 August Poruchik Loiko was on patrol with squadronmates Suk in Vickers FB 19 No 12 and Starshyi Unter-Officer Sapozhnikov in Nieuport 17 N1445 when, over Islovăž village, a Hansa-Brandenburg reconnaissance biplane was seen. After a combined attack the machine descended trailing smoke until it landed behind enemy lines near Rădăuţi. Reserve pilot Oblt George Altadonna and observer Oblt Adalbert Kuncze of *Flik* 40 survived this action unscathed.

The Rumanian Front weekly summary of 19 September 1917 reported that Poruchik Loiko shot down enemy aircraft on 11 September. That same day, according to Austrian records, a Hansa-Brandenburg C I of *Flik* 38, crewed by observer Ltn Daroczy and pilot Stefan Szöllöczy, was shot down by a Russian fighter while undertaking aerial photography. During the combat the observer was fatally wounded in the stomach, but the pilot managed to land the damaged aeroplane on his own airfield. This aircraft was claimed by Loiko as his sixth, and last, victory.

Poruchik Ivan Loiko's wartime decorations included the Order of St Anne 4th Class with the legend 'For Bravery', the Order of St Anne 3rd Class with Swords and Bow, the Order of St Anne 2nd Class with Swords, the Order of St Stanislav 3rd Class with Swords and Bow, the Order of St Stanislav 2nd Class with Swords, the Order of St Vladimir 4th Class with Swords and Bow and the Order of the Star of Rumania.

During the Russian Civil War of 1918-20 Loiko was an active participant in the White movement, having joined the ranks of the Volunteer Army in December 1918. That year he was promoted to Kapitan and, on 30 September 1919, he rose to the rank of polkovnik. Serving in the staff of Gen Wrangel's Russian Army, Loiko participated in the famous defeat of numerous Red Army cavalry groups of the 1st Cavalry Corps under the command of Dmitry Zhloba. In that operation, pilots of the White Army constantly attacked the Red Army cavalry with bombs and machine gun fire.

In late November 1920 Loiko was evacuated from the Crimea along with Wrangel's troops. From 1921 he served as an instructor in the Kingdom of Yugoslavia Air Force's flying school in Novi Sad. In 1923 Loiko returned to the Soviet Union in an unusual manner – flying across the Rumanian-Soviet border in a hijacked Yugoslavian Air Force Breguet XIX together with former White Army pilot Pavel Kachan. During 1924-29 Loiko served in the Red Army Air Forces as an instructor in the 2nd Flying School in Borisoglebsk.

In 1929 Loiko was accused of espionage on behalf of Rumania. In accordance with article 58-6 of the criminal code, the board of the OGPU (*Ob'edinennoe Gosudarstvennoe Politicheskoe Upravlenie* – Joint State Political Directorate) sentenced him to ten years' deprivation of liberty. Loiko worked as a prisoner on the Vaygach expedition mounted by the OGPU/NKVD (*Narodnyy Komissariat Vnutrennikh Del* – People's Commissariat for Internal Affairs). Vaygach Island is situated in the Arctic, between the Barents and Kara Seas, and lead-zinc ore was extracted from there in large quantities in 1934-38. In 1934 Loiko was granted an early discharge, and worked as a civilian in the Vaygach mining trust. His fate after 1936 is unknown – there is a strong possibility that he committed suicide in April of that same year, but this information is unreliable.

Ivan Loiko in the 1920s, this photograph having also been taken in Yugoslavia after his emigration to the Balkans

OTHER ACES

Evgraf Kruten

The son of a gentleman by birth, Colonel Evgraf Kruten was born in Kiev on 17 December 1890. In 1911 he graduated from Konstantin Artillery School with the rank of podporuchik. After serving in artillery units for two years he managed to transfer to aviation. In August 1913 Kruten was sent to the 3rd KAO to train as an officer-observer. A year later Kruten graduated from Gatchina Military Flying School and was given the title of military pilot.

With the onset of the war he left for the front with the 21st KAO. In March 1915 he was transferred to the 2nd Army aviation detachment (Army AO), and from May 1916 Kruten was appointed commander of that squadron. On 24 May 1916 his appointment as commander of the redesignated 2nd AOI was confirmed. Later that year he was sent to France with other Russian pilots to study the Allies' combat experience and master new fighter types. Posted to Pau airfield in January 1917, Kruten was later transferred to a flying school at Cazau. In early February he was assigned to the famous *Escadrille* N3 of the aviation group led by Capitaine Felix Brocard, and Kruten completed combat missions over Amiens and Nancy.

Returning to Russia in March 1917, he wrote several booklets devoted to the tactics of air combat, entitled *Invasion of Foreigners, First Theories in Fighting Aviation, Manual of the Fighter Pilot, Types of Fighter Aircraft, Creation of Fighter Groups, Air Combat, Military Aviation of France* and *Glaring Necessities of Russian Aviation*.

On 18 April 1917 Kruten was appointed commander of the 2nd BAG of the Southwest Front, which incorporated the 3rd, 7th and 8th KAOs. The group was based at an airfield near Plotychy village at that time.

By then Kruten had engaged the enemy in the air on a number of occasions over the previous two years. His first clash came on 21 February 1915 during his service in the 2nd Army AO, the future ace flying non-fighter-like Voisin LA pusher biplane No 42 at the time. Kruten had taken off with observer Kapitan of General Staff Leon Dusimetier for a long-range reconnaissance along the Sochaczew-Ravka route. Staying aloft for four hours and ten minutes, they dropped six bombs on the 49th Division. During the course of the mission they came across an enemy aeroplane and attacked it, Dusimetier opening fire with his rifle. The enemy two-seater subsequently descended at a steep angle. On 26 March Kruten was awarded the Order of St Anne 4th Class with the inscription 'For Bravery' for shooting down a German aeroplane.

On 4 July 1915 military pilot Poruchik Kruten and observer Shtabs-Kapitan Kazakov attacked a hostile aeroplane in the region of Novogeorgievsk. During the fight Kazakov fired 96 rounds from his machine gun, and the enemy aircraft was seen to lose height as it flew back behind German lines.

Five-victory ace Kapitan Evgraf Kruten, commander of the 2nd BAG in 1917

Kruten's first effective combat took place on 30 July 1916 after he had taken off from Malevo airfield in Nieuport 11 N1137/1582 in pursuit of a German Albatros C III. Seeing his foe over Svoyatichi, he fired off a solitary drum of ammunition at the aeroplane. While Kruten was rearming his Lewis machine gun, he lost sight of the enemy aircraft and returned to his airfield. It later transpired that Kruten's bullets had broken the C III's petrol pipe near the carburettor and severed a control cable. The German pilot, Alfred Heizelmann, made a forced landing within the 9th AK's defensive positions and was captured, as was his observer, Willenbucher. C III No 422 (fitted with 160 hp Mercedes engine wk-nr 25221) of *Flieger Abteilung* 31, based at an airfield near the villages of Derewianczhce and Pronchaki, was handed over to the 2nd KAO in good order. In December 1916 it was sent to the Lebedev aircraft factory in Petrograd to be copied.

Two days after Kruten had claimed his first victory he downed a second German aircraft. Having taken off from Malevo airfield in N1137/1582, at 0800 hrs he noticed shell bursts over Pogorel'tsy. After gaining altitude over Zamirye Station he succeeded in cutting off his opponent's escape route to the frontline. Kruten recalled, 'The German pilot tried to break through by diving beneath me, but I shot away one drum at him'. Over Nesvizh Kruten attacked for the second time, from head-on, and used up his second, and last, drum.

With his ammunition spent he had to resort to threatening manoeuvres to force his opponent to descend to 1400 m (4600 ft). Kruten saw that the engine of the enemy machine had stopped, and steam was escaping

Kruten sits on a propeller blade from downed Hansa-Brandenburg C I 64.55 of *Flik* 18, which he shot down on 24 May 1917 near Marianka village for his fifth, and last, victory

from its radiator. The aircraft came down near Nesvizh, at which point Cossacks made a timely appearance and prevented the crew from burning their machine, taking them prisoner. The pilot, Fw Hoffmann, had been wounded in his neck and arm, but the observer, Oblt Henning von Oertzen, was uninjured. Kruten circled over the site and then returned to his airfield. It turned out that he had shot down Rumpler two-seater No 615 also from *Flieger Abteilung* 31. The aircraft was not badly damaged, and it was later used by the 1st KAO.

In May-June 1917 Kapitan Kruten added a further three victories to his tally, all of which were claimed at the controls of new Nieuport 17 N2232, powered by 110 hp Le Rhône engine No 3584 and armed with a Lewis machine gun on the upper wing.

The first of these successes came at 0750 hrs on 18 May when Kruten closed on a Hansa-Brandenburg C I that was conducting a reconnaissance of Tarnopol at an altitude of 4000 m (13,000 ft) to the northeast of Brzeżany. After his first attack the enemy machine began to fall away until a wing broke off and it caught fire. The aircraft crashed near Vymyslovka, some 27 km (17 miles) west of Tarnopol. Only wreckage of the burned aircraft was found, plus a 200 hp Fiat engine, two Schwarzlose machine guns and the burnt corpses of its crew. There were ten bullet holes in the engine, petrol tank and radiator. The remains of the crew were later buried with military honours. According to Austrian archives the aircraft was Brandenburg C I 69.78, crewed by pilot Kpl Drenk and observer Oblt Baron von Kutschera of *Flik* 18. On 20 May Russian pilots dropped a letter in French over the enemy rear, telling of the death of the Baron and his pilot.

Three days later, again near Tarnopol, Kapitan Kruten twice attacked an enemy reconnaissance aeroplane. The Russian reported that the observer in the aircraft was killed, as he stopped firing and fell to the cockpit floor. The engagement had taken place at 0630 hrs at an altitude of 3000 m (9800 ft), after which the pilot descended steeply to 1500 m (4900 ft) with the engine running and flew away over the German trenches. The *Casualty List of German Air Forces During World War 1* records that on 23 May 1917 Ltn Erich Pütter was killed in action. Called up for military service in aviation from *Feld Artillerieregiment* 40, he was flying from an airfield in Jezierna (Galicia), not far from Tarnopol, when he perished.

On 6 June 1917 Kruten was returning from a flight when his Nieuport 17 N2232 suddenly went into a spin from a height of just 20-30 m (65-100 ft) and crashed on Plotychy airfield, killing the Russian ace. Quickly removed from the wreckage of the aeroplane, he died in the arms of his comrades

On 24 May, when his fuel was running out after a two-hour patrol over Tarnopol, Kruten saw three Hansa-Brandenburg C Is and attacked one of them at 1500 m (4900 ft) east of Denisov Station. He had to make his attack in a gliding descent, as his fuel was spent. Nevertheless, Kruten managed to wound the pilot and observer, and the C I made a forced landing among Russian troops near Marianka. Landing nearby, Kruten found that he had shot down C I 64.55 of *Flik* 18. Its crew, pilot Kpl Anton Lager and Ltn d R Willibald Patzelt, were captured, but Lager, who was seriously wounded, later died.

On 6 June Kruten was returning from a flight when his Nieuport 17 suddenly went into a spin from a height of just 20-30 m (65-100 ft) and crashed on Plotychy airfield, killing the Russian ace. Removed from the wreckage of the aeroplane, he died in the arms of his comrades.

His exploits in combat had earned Kruten the Order of St Stanislav 3rd Class, the Order of St Vladimir 4th Class with Crossed Swords and Bow, the Order of St George 4th Class, the Order of St Stanislav 2nd Class with Crossed Swords, the Gold Sword for Bravery and the French *Croix de Guerre*. He was buried in Luk'yanovskoe Cemetery in Kiev.

Konstantin Vakulovsky

Konstantin Vakulovsky was born into a family of gentry – his father was a major general – on 15 October 1894 in Dagestan, in the Caucasus. In 1914 he graduated from Nikolaevskoe Military Engineering School, and from 8 August 1915 he served as an observer in the Novogeorgievsk Fortress Aviation Detachment, with whom he learned to fly. Order No 446 of the Supreme Commander in Chief, dated 31 May 1915, conferred upon Vakulovsky the title of military pilot. Such an accolade was usually only awarded after graduation from a flying school, but an exception was made in Vakulovsky's case because he displayed such natural abilities. He completed 50 educational flights without an instructor in the detachment and passed his examination flight with distinction.

In October 1915 Vakulovsky was transferred to the 33rd KAO. On 14 June 1916 he flew captured Albatros No 400 on a reconnaissance flight and was attacked by a Fokker E III fighter, its pilot opening fire at 500 m (550 yd) and then turning towards Schönberg, flying on a parallel course. Twenty-five minutes later another Fokker scout appeared, and the enemy

Flanked by fellow fighter pilots, Shtabs-Kapitan Konstantin Vakulovsky, commander of the 1st AOI, sits on the wheel of his Morane-Saulnier Type I MS741 in the spring of 1917. On 1 April that year he used this aircraft to shoot down a Schneider-type enemy aeroplane from *Flieger Abteilung* 25 near Budslav Station

pilots tried in vain to shoot down the Albatros without crossing their own trench lines. It was Vakulovsky's first encounter with the enemy.

On 22 July 1916 he was appointed commander of the 1st AOI, and on 26 August, flying Nieuport 11 N1295, Vakulovsky attacked an enemy aeroplane. After his second firing pass the hostile aircraft continued to descend in a steep banking turn towards Kvakshta Lake. Vakulovsky did not see the point of impact.

He engaged German reconnaissance aircraft four times on 15 October 1916. On the last occasion he pursued an Albatros, and after three attacks it dived towards its own positions. Vakulovsky's Nieuport had been damaged during the combat, however, and he crashed as he landed at his airfield.

On 1 April 1917, commander of the 1st AOI Poruchik Vakulovsky, flying Morane-Saulnier Type I MS741, shot down a Schneider-type enemy aeroplane, fitted with a 200 hp Benz engine, near Budslav Station. The aircraft burnt out after it had crashed, killing the crew. The *List of German Air Force Casualties During World War 1* records that pilot Uffz Arthur Wolf and observer Ltn d R Hans Rusche of *Flieger Abteilung* 25 perished on this date in the Wileika region.

Having nearly finished photographing the third line of enemy trenches on 1 June, Vakulovsky was shelled by anti-aircraft artillery near Baldohn. At 500 m (1600 ft), fuel leaking from a damaged tank caught fire, and in seconds his aircraft was enveloped in flames. Vakulovsky managed to glide down and land on Dalen Island, where he was shelled by German artillery. Despite shell-shock, burns and wounds, he managed to escape from the burning aeroplane.

At 1945 hrs on 8 August Shtabs-Kapitan Vakulovsky flew a patrol in Nieuport 17 N1450, built by the Dux factory. Near Tuckum he found two enemy aircraft (described as fighters in the division's report) and attacked one of them. The other avoided action and flew away towards the sea. Vakulovsky attacked his target three times, firing at point-blank range, whereupon the German aeroplane went into a spin and crashed into the Gulf of Riga opposite the Pleenes-Tseems Islands. The Russian pilot followed the machine down to 500 m (1600 ft) and noticed a column of water at its point of impact.

Taken at the same time as the previous image, Vakulovsky (this time standing in the cockpit) and his men surround Type I MS741 for a 1st AOI group photograph

During his return flight Vakulovsky attacked a second pair of aircraft, approaching close to one of them and firing off half a drum before his machine gun jammed. After the attack the enemy aeroplane descended steeply in the Kavgern-Assern region and was lost to sight. It was covered in white linen, had two red and black stripes on its wings and fuselage and was armed with two machine guns.

Vakulovsky was involved in several combats on 19 August. At 1330 hrs he took off for a reconnaissance mission along the route Oger River-Kurtenhof farmstead-Uexküll in Nieuport 23 N3747. He shot down two aeroplanes during the course of the flight, one of which fell on Russian territory in the region of Uexküll. Other pilots of the 1st AOI saw the aircraft lying in a meadow near Uexküll Station. The second aircraft brought down by Vakulovsky fell in enemy territory.

In October 1917 he asked to be given a Sopwith Triplane as a reward for his combat achievements, as a small number of these machines had been delivered to the 1st AD depot. Vakulovsky subsequently perished in a flying accident in the summer of 1918.

For outstanding combat service Vakulovsky was decorated with the Order of St Anne 4th Class For Bravery, the Order of St Anne 3rd Class with Crossed Swords and Bow, the Order of St Anne 2nd Class with Crossed Swords, the Order of St Stanislav 3rd Class with Crossed Swords and Bow, the Order of St Stanislav 2nd Class with Crossed Swords, the Order of St Vladimir 4th Class with Crossed Swords and Bow, the Order of St George 4th Class, the Gold Sword for Bravery and the French *Croix de Guerre*.

Alexander Pishvanov

Born in Novocherkassk on 21 October 1893, Alexander Pishvanov was awarded Aviator's Certificate No 190 after finishing his training at the Odessa Aero Club in October 1913. At the beginning of World War 1 he volunteered for the army and served in the cavalry until mid-1915, being decorated with all four soldier's Crosses of St George for his heroism.

In the summer of 1915 Pishvanov insisted on being transferred to aviation, and he was duly sent to the Sevastopol Military Flying School in the autumn to train as a pilot. On 28 January 1916 Pishvanov completed his training on the Farman F 22 pusher and transferred to the Simferopol section of the school to be taught how to fly the Voisin pusher biplane by pilot-instructor Podpraporshchik Ionin. He completed this training on 26 March 1916, and the following month he graduated from Sevastopol Flying School with the rank of Starshyi Unter-Officer.

In early May 1916 Pishvanov was transferred to the 27th KAO. On 11 June he and observer Podporuchik Ivanov took off on a reconnaissance mission in Voisin V467 from an airfield near Yahimovshchizna. During the course of their flight they attacked an enemy Albatros at 2000 m (6500 ft) over Krevo-Kamenka, opening fire at short range. The enemy pilot descended rapidly and flew away to the rear of his lines.

After two months of active combat Pishvanov was transferred to Moscow Military Flying School to train on fighters. Upon completion of his conversion course, Pishvanov was assigned to the 10th AOI on 7 August. Attached to the 10th Army, the new fighter squadron was based at Gnidava airfield near Volyn, on the Southwest Front. The pilots of the 10th AOI patrolled in the region of Torshin-Zaturtsy-Rozhyshche-Kiselin,

Pishvanov usually flying single-seat Nieuport 9s N846 or N709, armed with a Lewis machine gun. Making his first operational flight on 2 October 1916, Pishvanov undertook patrols, photo-reconnassaince missions and escorted aircraft from other detachments.

In December 1916 the 10th AOI was transferred to Galaži, in Rumania, where its pilots flew in protection of the boat bridges on the River Danube. There was no aerial combat during this period.

By early March 1917 Pishvanov had flown 50 patrols totalling more than 80 hours of flying time. On 21 March he attacked an enemy reconnaissance aircraft over Galaži. Performing a wing-over, he brought his Nieuport 21 N1890 (with which he would make all of his aerial claims) in behind the enemy aircraft and opened fire at a range of less than 30 m (33 yd), wounding the observer. He pursued his quarry up to the frontline, where Russian pilots from the 29th KAO joined the combat. Together, they forced the pilot of the two-seater to crash-land in enemy-held territory. The victory was confirmed by Russian troops.

On 28 March Pishvanov and Rumanian pilot Cranu attacked a German Aviatik at an altitude of 3200 m (10,500 ft) south of Galaži. They made six attacks, by the end of which the enemy aeroplane was trailing black smoke. It dived towards Brăila and crash-landed in Beldoneżti. Soon after this engagement Pishvanov was promoted to Praporshchik.

On 15 April he and an unidentified Rumanian pilot made the first attack on a hostile aircraft in the Sireth River region. Later, Pishvanov attacked the same aircraft again on his own over Brăila, firing at it from close range until the two-seater entered a steep dive and landed.

In May the 10th AOI was attached to the 6th AD, which was itself part of the 6th Russian Army in Rumania.

On 26 June Pishvanov intercepted a group of four enemy aeroplanes at 4300 m (14,000 ft) over Ivežti. One machine broke away and headed for home when Pishvanov's machine gun jammed during his first attacking pass. Having cleared the jam, he resumed the fight. Although the three remaining enemy aircraft were now in a close formation, he again attacked one of them. As his Nieuport passed near the group, one of the enemy observers threw four grenades, which exploded in the air with huge puffs of white smoke.

At that point two French fighters arrived to support Pishvanov, one from Galaži and another from Tecuci. Together, they attacked one of the enemy aeroplanes and damaged it, the machine descending rapidly towards Putna. The three fighters then split up and attacked the two remaining aircraft. After Pishvanov opened fire on his target a grenade was again thrown at him and his prey escaped. In all, the Russian had made seven attacks.

Pishvanov's fourth confirmed victory occurred on 4 July 1917, during a patrol that resulted in five consecutive combats. The last took place over the Sireth River, near Endependanze. At a range of less than 40 m (44 yd), Pishvanov surprised the enemy crew with his machine gun fire, which hit the fuselage, engine and possibly the observer. The latter returned a burst of fire and then disappeared into his cockpit. Moments later the enemy pilot lost control and crash-landed on a farm within enemy territory. For this combat Pishvanov was nominated for the Order of St Vladimir 4th Class with Swords and Bow.

Five-victory ace Alexander Pishvanov seen in the late 1920s, after emigrating to the USA. Finding work as an engineer in the Sikorsky company shortly after his arrival in the west, he became an American citizen in 1928. In 1931 Pishvanov joined the Seversky Aircraft Corporation. He passed away on 6 August 1964

Austrian archives record that pilot Oblt Rupert Terk and observer Oblt Josef Brunner, both from *Flik* 36, were flying Hansa-Brandenburg C I 68.54 over Endependanze when they were attacked and shot down after a brief combat. Their attacker's fire damaged the C I's propeller and cooling system, and the pilot made a forced landing behind the Austrian trenches.

On the morning of 7 July Pishvanov attacked a group of enemy aeroplanes that were spotting artillery fire in the region of Latinul village. Accompanied by Podporuchik Desino, Pishvanov drove the machines back over enemy territory. Later, flying alone, Pishvanov attacked a twin-engined aircraft at an altitude of 4400 m (14,400 ft). He chased it down to 1200 m (3900 ft), at which point the Russian hit the machine hard with a burst of machine gun fire at point-blank range. The aircraft fell near the second line of trenches, where it was shelled by Russian artillery units. For this combat Pishvanov was nominated for the Order of St George 4th Class.

Two days later, by Order No 599 of the Supreme Commander-in-Chief, dated 9 July 1917, Pishvanov was conferred with the title of military pilot.

On 11 July Pishvanov encountered a hostile aeroplane in the region of Tutor-Vladimiresku. Attacking it from above, he opened fire at short range but his gun jammed. The enemy took this opportunity to return fire, and a bullet hit Pishvanov's right hand. In spite of the wound, and his faulty machine gun, Pishvanov did not break off the chase. Removing the jammed bullet case, he attacked the enemy machine and forced its pilot to withdraw to his own territory. Pishvanov returned to his airfield, where he damaged his Nieuport whilst landing. After this combat N1890 went to the 1st Aviation Depot for repair.

On 5 September Pishvanov received new Nieuport 17 N4191, and he flew this machine during September-October 1917. At the end of the year he was promoted to Poruchik.

In December Pishvanov flew to Novocherkassk and joined the Volunteer Army under the command of Gens Mikhail Alekseev and Anton Denikin. During the Russian Civil War Pishvanov fought against the Red Army, flying a Sopwith Camel fighter from the summer of 1919. His 6th aviation detachment of the VSYuR fought with distinction during the summer offensive on Moscow, a fact recorded in an order issued by the commander of the 1st Volunteer Corps, Lt Gen Alexander Kutepov.

After the White Army's retreat in the winter/spring of 1919/20, the 6th aviation detachment ended up in Grozny, where it was encircled by Red Army units and detachments of Chechen rebels. To escape captivity, in March 1920 Pishvanov and his comrades flew to Georgia in their Camels. There, they joined the Georgian Army, and also found employment with the Tiflis motor car company. However, independent Georgia was occupied by units of the 11th Red Army a year later and ceased to exist. Pishvanov travelled through Iran and eventually reached Great Britain, serving for some time as a pilot-instructor in the RAF.

Pishvanov emigrated to the USA in 1926 and worked as an engineer in the Sikorsky company. He became an American citizen in 1928, and in 1931 joined the Seversky Aircraft Corporation. Alexander Pishvanov passed away on 6 August 1964.

1

Nieuport 23 N3371 of Shtabs-Kapitan Sergey Sykhin, 22nd KAO of the 3rd BAG, Tatarshchina airfield, Minsk, Western Front, August 1917

The 22nd KAO received this French-built machine on 10 August 1917. By 1 November it had amassed 14 hours and 15 minutes of combat flying time. Its pilot, Sergey Sykhin, commanded the 22nd KAO from February 1917 until he was demobilised from the Russian Army in October 1917.

2

Nieuport 23 N3216 of Podporuchik Konstantin Krauze, 8th AOI, Novoselitse airfield, Chernovtsy, southwest Ukraine, October 1917

Built in France and delivered to Moscow in July 1917, this fighter was sent to the front in September. It was issued to the 8th AOI on 12 October, where it was routinely flown by Podporuchik Konstantin Krauze. He had joined the 8th AOI in May 1917, and served with the unit until he was demobilised six months later.

3

SPAD VII S1414 of Poruchik Ivan Kezhun, 8th KAO of the 2nd BAG, Bubnovka airfield, Tarnopol, Galicia, autumn 1917

The 8th KAO received this aeroplane on 12 September 1917, and Ivan Kezhun (who had been one of five Russian fighter pilots sent to France to gain combat experience in November 1916) flew it until mid-November. Later, the SPAD was on the strength of the Red Army Air Forces, being used in the Civil War. From December 1922 S1414 served with the fighter detachment of the 1st KAO until it was written off in 1923. In the wake of the October 1917 Revolution, Kezhun joined the Bolsheviks and participated in the Civil War as a military pilot with the 6th AOI of the Red Army Air Forces. He was dismissed from the latter in 1920, however.

4

Nieuport 23 N3598 of Poruchik Boris Guber, 19th KAO of the 1st BAG, Dunaevtsy airfield, Kamenets-Podolsk, Southwest Front, September 1917

The 19th KAO added this aircraft to its inventory on 16 August 1917. By 1 November 1917 it has flown 27 hours and 45 minutes in combat. The Christian symbol of immortality, 'Adam's head' (the skull and crossbones) was painted on its fin. In November 1917 the aeroplane was captured by Austro-Hungarian troops. Poruchik Boris Guber served in the 19th KAO until war's end, having flown as wingman to a number of Russia's leading aces. In November 1917 he was demobilised from the Russian Army.

5

Sikorsky S-16 s/n 201 of Kornet Yury Gilsher, 7th AOI, Yablonov airfield, Southwest Front, spring 1916

This product of Russian designer Igor Sikorsky was armed with a synchronised Vickers machine gun. It was one of three S-16s issued to the 7th AOI on 30 March 1916, and future five-victory ace Yury Gilsher flew the aircraft until 27 April when it was destroyed in a crash shortly after he had downed an Aviatik B III.

6

Moska-Bystritsky MBbis s/n 7 of Podporuchik Ivan Orlov, 7th AOI, Buchach, Tarnopol, Southwest Front, May 1916

Italian-designed and Russian-built, the MBbis had a Lewis gun mounted so as to shoot over the propeller due to its lack of synchronisation gear. One of 50+ examples built, s/n 7 was issued to the 7th AOI on 27 April 1916. Used by future five-victory ace Ivan Orlov to down a Lloyd C II on 26 May, the aircraft was written off as worn out in October of that same year.

7

Nieuport 21 N1810 of the 19th KAO of the 1st BAG, Dobrovody airfield, Podhaice, Southwest Front, May 1917.

The 19th KAO received this fighter on 18 November 1916, N1810 having a single Lewis machine gun mounted on its upper wing. Kokorin gained his fourth and fifth victories (two Hansa-Brandenburg C Is) in this machine in May 1917. He was killed at the controls of N1810 on 16 May 1917 when he was struck by an armour-piercing bullet almost certainly fired by German pilot Ltn Grybski of *Flieger Abteilung* 242.

8

Morane-Saulnier Type G MS316 of Poruchik Alexander Kozakov, 4th KAO, Guzov airfield, Northwest Front, March 1915

Russia's future 'ace of aces' Alexander Kozakov collected this machine from the Dux aircraft factory in Moscow in November 1914. On 18 March 1915 he rammed a German Albatros two-seat reconnaissance aircraft with it, seriously damaging MS316 in the process. The aircraft was duly repaired, and it remained in service until written off in August 1916.

9

Nieuport 10 N222 of Shtabs-Rotmistr Alexander Kozakov, 19th KAO, Dvinsk airfield, North Front, early summer 1916

Flown with great success by Kozakov, this Nieuport 10 was unusual in that it was armed with a captured German Maxim IMG 08 7.92 mm Spandau machine gun. The ace flew this aircraft from December 1915 to November 1917, amassing 49 hours and 20 minutes of combat flying time during this period. Kozakov shot down five enemy two-seat reconnaissance aircraft with N222, whilst a sixth possible success went unconfirmed.

10

Nieuport 10 N222 of Rotmistr Alexander Kozakov, 1st BAG, Dunaevtsy airfield, Southwest Front, September 1917

N222 survived long enough in service for it to be overhauled, repainted silver and adorned with the emblem of the 1st BAG on its rudder. Kozakov claimed his successes with this veteran machine between 14 June 1916 and 7 June 1917.

11

Nieuport 17 N1910 of Rotmistr Alexander Kozakov, 1st BAG, Kovalyuvka airfield, Southwest Front, spring 1917

Kozakov started flying this aircraft alongside N222 from December 1916, N1910 also being adorned with the 1st BAG's

'Adam's head' emblem – the symbol of death and fearlessness. He would claim eight victories with N1910, which had accrued 153 hours and 50 minutes of combat time by November 1917.

12
SPAD VII S1436 of Podpolkovnik Alexander Kozakov, 1st BAG, Dunaevtsy airfield, Southwest Front, October 1917
The 1st BAG received this machine on 29 August 1917, and Kozakov flew it from 14 October to late November 1917. He claimed his last victory with S1436 on 13 November 1917, when he helped fellow ace Ivan Smirnov force down a German reconnaissance aircraft in enemy territory. This success was never officially credited to Kozakov, however, being solely awarded to Smirnov instead. Later that same month S1436 was captured by Austro-Hungarian troops.

13
Nieuport 17 N1910 of Rotmistr Alexander Kozakov, 1st BAG, Kovalyuvka airfield, Southwest Front, late summer 1917
Like N222, N1910 survived long enough in the frontline to also be refurbished and repainted, as seen here. Aside from a patchy covering of gun metal grey paint overall, the fighter has had its 1st BAG motif reapplied in black rather than white and a full set of Imperial Military Air Fleet roundels added to the fuselage and wings.

14
Nieuport 10 N722 of Starshyi Unter-Officer Ivan Smirnov, 19th KAO of the 1st BAG, Lutsk, North Front, December 1916.
The 19th KAO of the 1st BAG received this aircraft on 28 August 1916, the two-seat Nieuport being armed with a solitary Colt machine gun for the observer. N722 was used by future ten-victory ace Ivan Smirnov to down his first enemy aeroplane on 20 December 1916, the Aviatik C-type being hit by fire from observer Shtabs-Kapitan Pentko. The pair had previously attacked two German reconnaissance aircraft in N722 on 20 September. The Nieuport 10 survived in frontline service until it was finally written off in June 1917.

15
Morane-Saulnier Type I MS740 of Praporshchik Ivan Smirnov, 19th KAO of the 1st BAG, Monastyrzhisko airfield, Galicia, Southwest Front, spring 1917
The 19th KAO took delivery of this aircraft on 29 November 1916 and applied the 1st BAG emblem on the fighter's rudder shortly thereafter. Smirnov claimed an Albatros C-type with MS740 for his second victory on 19 April 1917, having made four attacking passes at an enemy aircraft in this machine exactly two weeks earlier – the Morane was holed by return fire during the latter engagement. MS740 was written off in June 1917.

16
Nieuport 17 N2522 of Praporshchik Ivan Smirnov, 19th KAO of the 1st BAG, Gorodok airfield, Galicia, Southwest Front, August 1917
Smirnov flew Nieuport 17 N2522 from 22 June 1917, gaining three confirmed and two unconfirmed victories with it between 1 and 30 August. He had flown 27 sorties during August 1917, mostly in N2522, for a total flying time of 56 hours – he was the first pilot in the 19th KAO to attain such high figures.

17
SPAD VII S1546 of Praporshchik Ivan Smirnov, 19th KAO of the 1st BAG, Dunaevtsy airfield, Galicia, Southwest Front, autumn 1917
Smirnov began flying this fighter on 6 September 1917, and he continued to use it until war's end. He claimed six victories with S1546, five of which were officially confirmed.

18
Nieuport 17 N2453 of Poruchik Donat Makijonek, 7th AOI, Vikturovka airfield, Kozovo-Brzeżany, Southwest Front, summer 1917
The 7th AOI took delivery of this aeroplane from the 7th AD on 1 June 1917, and it was used in combat up to November of that year. Personal insignia was painted on its fuselage and tail. The fighter's ultimate fate is unknown. Makijonek was its first assigned pilot, and he flew it until September, when N2453 was passed on to Podporuchik Nyukyanen. Its total combat flying time was 94 hours and 15 minutes.

19
Nieuport 21 N1514/1941 of Podporuchik Ivan Orlov, 7th AOI, Vychulki airfield, Brzeżany, Southwest Front, autumn 1916
French-built N1514/1941 was delivered to the 7th AOI on 7 September 1916 already camouflaged in Western Front dark brown and greyish green. Initially flown by future five-victory ace Ivan Orlov, the scout was armed with a captured unsynchronised German Bergman MG 15 7.92 mm machine gun on its upper wing. Soon passed on to Podporuchik Bychkov, N1514/1941 was eventually written off in a crash in June 1917.

20
Nieuport 11 N1232 of Praporshchik Vasily Yanchenko, 7th AOI, Tysmenitsa airfield, Bohorodczany-Stanisławów, Southwest Front, spring 1917
Also supplied in French Aviation Militaire camouflage, this aircraft was issued to the 7th AOI on 21 July 1916. The fighter was fitted with a Hotchkiss M1914 machine gun on its upper wing. On 31 March 1917 Yanchenko used N1232 to down a Hansa-Brandenburg C I for his third of nine confirmed victories. This fighter was subsequently written-off in a crash on 27 July 1917 while being flown by Podporuchik Sakovich.

21
Nieuport 23 N3374 of Poruchik Vasily Yanchenko, 32nd KAO, Zhishchintsy airfield, Gorodok-Husiatyn-Zbrizh, Galicia, autumn 1917
In September 1917 Yanchenko was transferred to the 32nd KAO, where, on the 8th of that month, he was given brand new Nieuport 23 N3374. He immediately had his personal insignia – a black shield – painted on the fighter's tail. Yanchenko claimed his final four victories with N3374, although only three of them were officially credited to him. The ace continued to fly this aeroplane until his demobilisation in November 1917.

22
Nieuport 11 N1109 of Poruchik Ivan Loiko, 9th AOI, Piatra-Roman airfield, Rumanian Front, December 1916
Built in Russia in the Dux aviation factory, this aircraft was delivered to the 9th AOI on 20 August 1916. Four months later, on 14 December, future six-victory ace Ivan Loiko claimed a Hansa-Brandenburg two-seater shot down whilst flying N1109. His victory was not officially confirmed, however. The fighter was written off in a crash in January 1917.

23
Nieuport 17 N1448 of Praporshchik Vladimir Strzhizhevsky, 9th AOI, Săuceşti airfield, Czick-Szereda Comăneşti, Rumanian Front, summer 1917

The 9th AOI received this French-built aeroplane, armed with a synchronised Vickers machine gun, on 14 June 1917. Three days later future five-victory ace Vladimir Strzhizhevsky used the fighter to down a Hansa-Brandenburg C I. He destroyed a second C I with N1448 on 5 July. It was passed on to fellow ace Podporuchik Loiko shortly thereafter, and he claimed six victories flying the aircraft (only four of these were confirmed, however). Finally, squadronmate Poruchik Zirgiladze was given N1448 in September 1917. By war's end the aircraft's total combat flying time was an impressive 158 hours and 35 minutes.

24
Morane-Saulnier Type I MS742 of Praporshchik Grigory Suk, 9th AOI, Săuceşti airfield, Kézdi-Vàsárhely-Ocna-Bacău, Rumanian Front, March 1917

Suk's aeroplane was delivered to the 9th AOI on 6 February 1917, where it was armed with a synchronised Vickers machine gun. On 13 March he forced down a Hansa-Brandenburg C I while at the controls of MS742. Deemed to be worn out by May, the monoplane fighter was placed in storage in the 6th Aviation Park.

25
Nieuport 21 N1719 of Praporshchik Grigory Suk, 9th AOI, Săuceăti airfield, Ocna-Bacău, Rumanian Front, July 1917

The 9th AOI took delivery of this French-built machine on 7 January 1917, the fighter being armed with an unsynchronised Lewis machine gun. Suk claimed his third victory with the aircraft on 27 July when he downed an Oeffag C III. N1719 was also flown by Podporuchiks Loiko and Osipov. On 22 September it was transferred to the 28th KAO.

26
Vickers FB 19 No 12 of Praporshchik Grigory Suk, 9th AOI, Fălticeni airfield, Arbore-Rădăuţi-Hadikfalva, Rumanian Front, August 1917

This aeroplane was delivered to the 9th AOI on 12 August 1917, and two days later Grigory Suk used it to force down a Hansa-Brandenburg C I. On 30 August he became an ace when he claimed another two-seater down behind enemy lines whilst flying No 12. The FB 19 featured Russian roundels in eight positions – on the rudder, fuselage and the upper and lower wings (two insignia on either side). The machine's total combat flying time was just 25 hours and five minutes when it was deposited for storage in the 6th Aviation Park in October 1917.

27
SPAD VII S1440 of Praporshchik Grigory Suk, 9th AOI, Solka airfield, Rădăuţi, Rumanian Front, September 1917

The 9th AOI received this aeroplane in September 1917, and Suk claimed his final three victories with it the following month. On 15 November 1917 Grigory Suk stalled S1440 over the airfield while coming in to land after completing a mission, the ace perishing in the subsequent crash. The fighter had accumulated just 25 hours and 50 minutes of flying time prior to being written off.

28
Nieuport 11 N1137/1582 of Poruchik Evgraf Kruten, 2nd AOI, Malevo airfield, Pogoreltsy-Nesvizh-Minsk, Western Front, July-August 1916

This French-built fighter, powered by 80 hp Le Rhône engine N3434, was sent to Russia in April 1916. The 2nd AOI received it in July of that year, the aircraft being assigned to the unit CO, Evgraf Kruten. He had his personal insignia (the head of a Russian epical hero) painted on the fuselage sides. Kruten claimed the first two of his five confirmed victories in N1137. In December 1916 this aircraft was deposited for storage in the 2nd Aviation Park in Smolensk.

INDEX